🌱 🌱 🌱 CAROL ANN DELANEY'S NATURAL-BORN talent for making music may be her only ticket out of Bainesville, Arkansas. Daughter of a Gypsy fortune-teller, Carol Ann desperately needs to believe in her "Gypsy luck" as she clings to a secret dream: *Ladies and Gentlemen, may I present the beautiful and famous star of country and western music, Miss Carlotta Dell!*

But the applause Carol Ann hears in her heart is nothing like the sneers of "Little Gyp!" that she hears in the corridors of Bainesville High School. Then one day, unexpectedly, Carol Ann is asked to sing in front of the whole school, and the roars of approval become real for the first time. And this time the spotlight feels just right.

As graduation approaches, everybody's pulling Carol Ann in different directions. Will Bellows, the handsome and cocky farmer's son, offers to marry Carol Ann so she can "settle down and have a decent life for a change." Mama's crystal ball reveals no stardom in her daughter's future, just a lot of heartache for having such highfalutin ideas. Only Jean McCaffrey, her music teacher, recognizes Carol Ann's special gift. Mrs. McCaffrey gives her the formal training she needs, and the caring she's never known.

Although Carol Ann figures she's got about one chance in a million of making it big in Nashville, the part of her that's Carlotta Dell feels differently. 'Cause Carlotta Dell knows beyond any doubt that there's just no end to the songs she can write or the notes she can reach.

Summer of My German Soldier
Philip Hall likes me. I reckon maybe.
Morning Is A Long Time Coming
Get on out of here, Philip Hall

BETTE GREENE

Them That Glitter

and

Them That Don't

ALFRED A. KNOPF
NEW YORK

Grateful acknowledgment is made to the following for permission to reprint previously published material:

Chappell Music Company: An Excerpt from the lyric of *Oklahoma* by Rodgers & Hammerstein. Copyright © 1943 by Williamson Music Co. Copyright Renewed. International Copyright Secured. All Rights Reserved. Used by permission.

Warner Bros. Music: An excerpt from the lyric of *When Irish Eyes Are Smiling* by Chauncey Olcott, Geol. Graff Jr. & Ernest R. Ball. © 1912 (Renewed) Warner Bros. Inc. All Rights Reserved. Used by permission.

The lyric of *Stood Up and Let Down* © 1983 by Laura Lee, Patsy Jane, Wendy Sue, and Bette Jean. All Rights Reserved. Used by permission.

THIS IS A BORZOI BOOK
PUBLISHED BY ALFRED A. KNOPF, INC.

Manufactured in the United States of America
1 3 5 7 9 0 8 6 4 2

Library of Congress Cataloging in Publication Data
Greene, Bette, 1934–
Them that glitter and them that don't.
Summary: Though she has always been told the contrary, a young Gypsy girl living in the rural South is convinced that she can use her singing talent to become someone really special.
[1. Gypsies—Fiction. 2. Parent and child—Fiction.
3. Country life—Fiction] I. Title.
PZ7.G8283Th 1983 [Fic] 82–13020
ISBN 0-394-84692-3 ISBN 0-394-94692-8 (lib. bdg.)

BKMB

This book is for
JORDAN JOSHUA GREENE
who loves ski slopes, trucks
with four-wheel drive, and
his mom and dad.

THEM THAT GLITTER
AND THEM THAT DON'T

1

❧ ❧ ❧ THE ANNUAL Dexter county fair in Bainesville, Arkansas, is always filled to the brim with suckers
who'll even wait in line if they have to just to get themselves fleeced. At least that's what my mother has been
saying since seven o'clock this morning when we set up
our old Army surplus tent on the dusty deserted fringe of
the fairgrounds.

3

This was the first time that Mama had officially been open for business since she left the circus—or, to be more accurate, since nineteen years ago when the circus left her. Still, I guess I was surprised at how thrilled she was when we unrolled her old moldy and mildewed canvas sign and safety pinned it across the tent's opening for all the world to read:

She Knows All! She Sees All!
The G*R*E*A*T
* * * PRINCESS ASTRIAL * * *
World's Greatest
Crystal Ball Reader

We hauled a card table with one rickety leg into the tent along with two metal folding chairs and a large grocery bag that held a few clothes but no groceries. And then finally my best friend, my beautiful nylon-stringed guitar.

Slipping out of the old denim work shirt that she had been wearing over her ankle-length flowered skirt, Mama, now totally bare chested, went rummaging through the bag.

I rushed to guard the entrance. "Jesus, Mama! Somebody could come in!"

She laughed now as she had so many times before at my modesty. "My daughter, how is it that you're such a prude? Surely even in Bainesville folks have seen boobs before." From the sack she dug out a beaded Gypsy blouse and slipped it over her head. "And are mine any different?"

4

I told myself, just go on helping her get ready for business and never mind answering her back. What we needed to do now was to make money, not fight. But then when she really was with the circus, none other than Pat Patterson himself used to give the sales pitch that would have folks clamoring for one of her readings. I threw the Indian print bedspread over the table, and there in the dead center placed the crystal ball that had once belonged to my mother's mother. The beautiful Lavita, wife to Victor Yergis, King of the Gypsies.

With the tips of four fingers she tapped the center of her chest. "Today, Carol Ann, we're going to land a rich mark. I can feel it here, here deep within my heart."

"I'd settle for a few not-so-rich ones," I told her. "The kids need milk, fresh fruit, meat, and vegetables every day. My home ec teacher says—"

"Your home ec teacher—ha!" said Mama, who began to laugh, but not from what you'd call pleasure. "What does that thin-lipped little gorgio know?"

"She's got her master's degree from Boston University in nutrition."

"Don't waste my time telling me what she's done copied from some book when the Princess Astrial knows what has never been trusted to the written word. The Princess knows all the secrets of the human heart. Generation after generation of secrets."

"Education is something that you have with you all your life," I said, parroting one of my teachers, but I couldn't for the life of me remember offhand just which one.

"Well, so is a mole," said Mama, pointing to the noticeable black circle near her lips. "But I don't know what good it does a person."

"If you're going to talk silly—"

"All right then, what about that Prescott girl?" asked Mama. "Started school the same time you did, and dropped out in the seventh grade to marry Larry Berber. Well, maybe she ain't got what you'd call a *real* education, but she sure has got something a whole lot better. A car with windows that go right up or down just by punching the right buttons."

I picked up my guitar and began to tune. I guess I just didn't know of a way to make her understand that *having* something wasn't the same thing as *being* something. As being somebody. Even now I still don't know exactly how to go about transforming myself from plain ole Carol Ann Delaney into the glamorous country and western star, Miss Carlotta Dell—except in my daydreams. Only thing is I know—I guess I know—that education, both regular and musical, has got to be part of the equation.

I went on about my business of fiddling with the E string, which tends to slip, while silently congratulating myself that we didn't get into one of our arguments. Mama was all the time wanting—maybe even needing—me to believe in her words and prophecies just like I used to when I was little. But I was no longer little, and so believing just seemed to all the time get harder and harder. But maybe if half my blood wasn't Irish blood, I'd have had an easier time of it. It's hard to know.

"Ma, what kind of songs do you think will sort of help folks get in the right mood to have a crystal ball reading?"

Mama's slate-black eyes turned down as they often do when she thinks, but when she did look up, it was clear that she had reached some sort of conclusion. "Oh, you were born knowing how to capture the attention of a crowd. You're not a Gypsy princess for nothing, you know. It's all in the blood. All of us Gypsies are born entertainers. It's one of the ways we manage to get by, Carol Ann, so I ain't worrying about you. You'll know what to do."

I tried for just that matter-of-fact tone which wouldn't let her know just how important this rare compliment was to me. "In that case, I think I'll begin by playing something lively and popular like "Yellow Submarine" and then I'll do a Negro spiritual or two, probably "Swing Low, Sweet Chariot," and that ought to get folks into a thoughtful enough mood so I can give them Princess Astral's sales pitch."

According to our plan, Mama stayed inside the tent whiie I went out front to attract a crowd. Trouble was, at nine o'clock on this already warm September morning there were only a few people milling around the fairgrounds. That ought to make standing up and singing easier, but it doesn't work that way. Standing up and singing without a single listener doesn't feel quite right. No righter than carrying on a conversation with yourself in a very public place.

So, strumming too softly to be noticed, I began playing the music to one of my own compositions. So far the music didn't have words, leastways no more words than the two-word title, "Wild Flower."

At a time when most every song you hear is either about love found or love lost, it must sound plumb silly to write a song in tribute to a single flower. 'Specially since people go around calling all free-growing flowers weeds.

7

Frankly, I can't too much understand anybody feeling that way, 'cause I look at it differently.

I mean, we all see greenhouse flowers that are raised under perfect growing conditions, and they are sure enough things of great beauty. But it's not until I see a living thing grow strong and beautiful and free in a dry and sandy soil that I feel my heart soar. And that's when I begin to feel that just maybe that's the greatest beauty of all.

Mama came through the tent's opening and looked around the still-empty grounds. "Ain't no fish around here for the catching. Let's go moseying about."

"Might as well," I said, adjusting my shoulder strap so that the guitar would hang from my back. As we ambled across the grounds, the few people who were about always seemed to give us a backward glance. I wasn't exactly sure if it was because we were Gypsies or because of Mama's miniature Indian bells that she wore around her neck, making her comings and goings such a musical event.

Mama wears her Indian bells because she believes that anything that comes from India is especially lucky, India being our ancestral home and all. Some people, even including my home ec teacher, Mrs. Helen Constant, thought that we were Egyptians.

"Oh, no ma'am," I once told her. "My ancestors just hung around Egypt so long that it gave a lot of folks that impression. We also liked Rumania and Hungary, Turkey, and Spain too, but we all the time kept on moving west. I have this theory that if we keep on moving west, then someday we'll have come full circle, back to India, our homeland."

8

Actually, if it wasn't for Mama—I mean my being known as my mama's daughter—then probably nobody would ever guess that I'm a Gypsy, too. Oh, my eyes are every bit as black as Mama's and my cheekbones are every bit as high, if that's possible. But my skin and brick-red hair come straight from Papa's Irish side of the family. The Delaney side. It's Papa who every once in a while looks me over closely before remarking: "You've got skin fair enough to put the prettiest colleen to shame!"

Although this may sound downright conceited to say, I'm not, by any stretch of the imagination, what you'd call bad-looking. And once I get money enough to buy something pretty to wear and a bottle of real sweet-smelling shampoo to use on my hair instead of laundry soap, then I honestly believe that I'm going to look a whole lot better.

I don't think that's one bit conceited to say, because when I get to be Carlotta Dell, I've got to be good-looking. Yes sir, Carlotta Dell's hair is going to be so silkily shiny that it'll dazzle the spotlights just like Carlotta is going to dazzle them with her songs. Songs so ripe with feelings that nobody'll go away untouched. That's a lot of what my dream of stardom means to me, being so good at singing and composing that I'm actually lending my eyes. Showing folks what it feels like to see what I see . . . and to feel what I feel.

❦ ❦ ❦

THE LARGEST AREA of the county fair was where the livestock was going to be exhibited inside an area circled by a whole cavalry of sawhorses. Lots of folks in these parts would up and die happy if they could manage

9

just once in their life to win a blue ribbon for one of their heifers or steers. Most of the time, though, the ribbons (blue, red, and white) were won by none other than Mr. Louis Leander Huntington, whose animals live in a barn so modern it seems way too good for any cow.

The chrome on the new lime-green fire truck was being polished to a fare-thee-well by Mr. Tom Hackett, who's been a volunteer member of our town's Fire Department longer than anybody can remember. I read that not long ago in the *Bainesville Weekly News*. And, incidentally, whether a fire truck ought to be painted lime green or red, like God intended, is presently one of the biggest arguments in town.

On past the basketball throws (three tries for a quarter) sponsored by the high school basketball team, and the flower exhibit sponsored by the ladies' flower club, and the bake sale sponsored by the Church of the Gospel Lighthouse, there was another vehicle on display almost as impressive to the onlookers as the fire truck: a brand new John Deere tractor.

My grandfather, Victor Yergis, like most Gypsies, preferred horses to tractors. Said they never need gas or expensive repairs. One time in the heat of the summer when we were caravaning up in the Ozarks, he gave his horse, Yankel, an affectionate pat and said, "A man don't need but two things in this world to be happy: A good wife and a good horse."

My own father, Charles—I still don't like it, and I guess I never will get used to everybody calling him by his nickname, Painter—is known to everybody in this town and probably even way beyond as Painter because of the work he did for twenty years. Painting, spraying is what he calls it, those stripes down the middle of the highway for the Arkansas Department of Public Works.

It's not fair, but everytime one of those lines veered off course, folks laughed and pointed and said that ole Painter must have had himself a few too many belts of booze.

Directly behind upturned Dr Pepper crates that served as a booth, a sign was being pounded into the ground by a heavily perspiring Reverend Bartlett. "Would you looky there at that sign!" said Mama, sounding truly amazed.

I read out loud: "Do you know where you're going to spend eternity?"

She slapped the side of her rump before exploding with laughter. "How's that for planning for the future?"

I asked, "If the Reverend Walter Bartlett had been ordained a priest instead of a minister, would you still laugh?"

"Ministers don't give no money when they baptize one of our new ones. But priests, they almost always got a handful of coins for a Gypsy baby."

"Is that why I was baptized so many times by so many different priests? Was it five times?"

"Hey!" said Mama like she does when she doesn't like the subject being discussed. "Would you smell that good food a-cooking!"

We both sucked in the air heavy with hamburgers charcoal broiling. "Now who in their right mind would eat hamburgers for breakfast?" I asked at the same time my stomach growled out its answer.

"I would!" answered Mama, while making a direct line for the food stand.

"We got us enough money for hamburgers?" I asked,

knowing that I was going to feel heavy disappointment if she said no, no money for hamburgers.

But instead she slapped her hand down hard on the makeshift counter as she sang out, "Two of your hamburgers, and don't be stingy with the onions!"

Mama and I found a grassy patch at the edge of the field and began eating our hamburgers slowly enough to make them last while we shared a single bottle of Orange Crush. "Now, ain't this the sweet life?" asked Mama, leaning back on her elbows. "Sitting out here in the warm September sun, eating restaurant food, and watching the world parade on by?"

"Sure is," I answered, feeling nice and warm and pleasantly filled. "Guess you surely must miss the sweet life you had when you were traveling all over with Pat Patterson's circus."

"Oh, yeah . . . know, every year we traveled through dozens of Arkansas towns: Hardy, Pocahontas, Russellville, Fayetteville, Arkadelphia, Pine Bluff, Parkin, Wynne, Osceola, El Dorado, Warren, Forrest City, Helena—bet I could still name them all if I had to." Mama sighed. "And during those early years when Pat was being good to me, it was as close to living the sweet life as anything I've ever known."

I was interested as I could be in everything about her life back then, but Pa surely wasn't. Sometimes when she talked about those years with Pat, my pa got mad. Maybe even a little jealous? He was all the time telling her that if Pat was so great, then how come he drugged her to within an inch of her life and then left her like a dying dog on the highway just north of town?

To be perfectly frank, I think Pa's question was a good one. I mean, how could one human person do that to another? And if Pa hadn't spotted her while spraying highway lines, she would've died. Died all alone like a mangy old dog. Can you imagine a stranger saving her from the man who swore for five years that he loved her?

I wish I could have seen Papa then. Holding her head in his strong arms while she took tiny sips of cool water from his thermos. Later he took her to his home and bathed her wounds before fixing her up with drugstore ointment.

Mama went on talking about Pat Patterson and all his previous lives on this earth. "Saw it all in the crystal ball, just as plain as I can see your face. It was Pat, known then as Thelonius, who brought a cup of water to Jesus' lips as he hung at Calvary. And 1,492 years later it was Pat, known then as the great Indian warrior Mirameecho, who stood at the edge of the waters to first welcome Christopher Columbus and his sailors to the new world."

I interrupted. "I'd like to ask you something."

"What?"

"Only if you promise first not to get mad."

"Me get mad?" She sounded so innocent as her mouth parted just enough to expose the left-of-center gold tooth with the heart-shaped cutout that Pat Patterson had bought for "his Gypsy" all those years ago, as a token of "love everlasting." "Hey, are you trying to strike a bargain with me, Carol Ann?"

"Well, what if I am?"

"Okay," she said, holding her hand up in a Boy Scout salute. "I won't get mad."

"Well, it's about all those things that you say you see

1 3

in the crystal ball. I mean if you can really and truly see all those things that you say you can, then why didn't you see that Pat was going to leave you behind when the circus left Bainesville?"

She picked up a crumb of hamburger bun from her flowered skirt and popped it into her mouth. "Know something? I thought you understood a lot more'n you do about the ball. It's like . . . like watching television. Some things show up on the screen and some things happen away from the camera's eye. Sometimes you watch one channel and not the other. Understand now?"

I didn't want her to even begin to suspect that I still had doubts, so I just nodded thoughtfully. Still, I felt sad for a time that would never come again. That innocent time when my love for Mama didn't leave room for a single doubt. Looking back, I think I understood now why I could almost always hold my head up even when my class-mates were taunting me with cries of "Little Gyp." Back then I really believed that nothing really bad could ever happen to me 'cause Mama would always be there. Always protecting me with her Gypsy magic.

If only I knew how to believe again . . . really believe. If I could just know that she would love me now like she did so long ago. But I can't, and I reckon that that's one of the problems between us. What's a person to do, though, when she can't find her way back to pretend? That lovely place where Mama and only Mama has the power to save me from fears real and fears imagined. Truth is, she'll never forgive me for letting go of make-believe and I'll never forgive her for hanging on to it.

Mama gave me a little poke with her elbow to let me

know that there was more coming. "But if you want to hear where I made my mistake, then okay, I'll tell you. In not getting Pat to marry me at the very beginning. He would have, too. That way when he tired of me, I would have been left with my alimony check instead of just bruises, cuts, five broken ribs, a stoned-out head, and," she said, pointing to the weatherworn canvas sign that framed our tent, "that there sign. Ask me and I'll tell you what living together is. Ain't nothing but horseshit, and any woman who lives with a man without him first marrying her is going to be living in horseshit!"

I handed Ma the last swig of Orange Crush and she drank it down, every last drop of it, before speaking again. "While I was in the tent alone, I saw a vision in the ball and when it comes true, then you'll have a world of trust again in your mama. Just like you did when you were a youngun."

"What did you see, Ma?"

"Money! Money! Money!" She said, wiggling her fingers. "On this very day a rich sucker will come into the tent. Remember what you are told here, because before this very sun goes down, a lot of money will have passed into these hands."

"You're sure?" I felt my own excitement rise. "You sure you actually saw that?!"

"Mark my words. 'Cause this day will never fade from your memory, Carol Ann. Not even when you yourself are an old lady and your mama here is resting with the angels will you ever forget this day!"

2

_____

🌱 🌱 🌱 IF THE RICH SUCKER was going to show, he was sure enough taking his own sweet time. It was already past three o'clock, and the few readings that Mama had given were for a buck, not a billion. Still, people would be milling around here just as long as the sun gave light, at least for the next three hours or so. And that's why I hadn't begun to give up hope, not by a long shot.

Mama had taken in somewhere between five and six dollars, and at today's prices that wouldn't buy much more'n a lot of pasta and a little cheese.

I pictured my home ec teacher, Mrs. Helen Constant, ending her last nutrition class with her stern-faced warning: "You all must eat something daily from each of the seven basic foods. And always remember, students, that if you don't take care of your body, then your body will *not* take care of you."

Standing here in front of our dusty tent with my guitar in the ready position, I was frightened to think that if Mrs. Constant was right, then all five of us Delaneys were every day, in every way, growing sicklier and sicklier.

But why did it always have to be my responsibility seeing to it that at least the kids ate right? Funny, it didn't make sense, but sometimes, maybe most of the time, I felt as though I was born to be the only true adult in this family.

Stop to think of it, I guess that's when I got the angriest at Ma. Not for something terrible that she did or said half so much as for something that she was. Or—to be more accurate—for something that she wasn't. I needed my mother to be that—a mother. A caring, seeing-to-every-thing, taking-charge mother. But the truth was she was at least half the time just another one of the kids. And for Papa that goes double.

Just the same, I was getting madder and madder with myself for not getting the big money to roll in. Was it my fault? All my fault? When Mama was with the circus, she says, people sometimes had to wait in line to have their fortune read by the great, all-seeing Princess Astrial.

And yet when I thought of my baby brother, my beautiful baby brother, Bubba Jay, at eighteen months teething on dog biscuits, I wanted to scream out, "It's not fair, but it's not all my fault either! So don't go blaming me if Pat Patterson knows better'n me how to get folks excited about fortune-telling!"

While I fiddled around with the slipped E string, I told myself that there was, at least, one thing I could do. I could stop holding myself back as far as my singing goes. Stop worrying about being shy . . . about my dignity. For once I had to stop fretting about whether or not I was standing out here making a fool of myself. People who eat from the basic seven can worry about things like that if they want to, but not me. That's one worry I sure as hell can't afford.

Suddenly I was singing. This time really singing, singing to myself about myself. That's all there was and there wasn't nothing else. At least nothing else that mattered.

People, first a few and then a few more, began gathering. Didn't care who came . . . who listened, or even who passed judgment. Not one way or the other. 'Cause the great singer-composer Carlotta Dell has her mind focused elsewhere. There inside those batty Beatles' world within a world. Their zany, joyful world of "The Yellow Submarine."

I'm singing as though there's nobody here who could laugh or ridicule. I'm singing as though there's only me, only God, and only this song. And for the first time today I'm singing straight from the heart.

Before the last note drifted away, there was clapping. Not just nice polite clapping either, but honest-to-God enthusiastic clapping. That's good, but it wasn't as though I *had* to have it. Not really. The few times in the past that I had sung before people was when I sat cross-legged in front of a roaring Gypsy bonfire. And even then I spent most of my time searching faces for signs of approval, but, like I said, that was all in the past. 'Cause I'm not Carol Ann, the Little Gyp, anymore, I'm me. I'm Carlotta!

As I played and sang the spiritual "Swing Low, Sweet Chariot," my voice had a low, sweet, and yet sad sound because I was thinking about how it must feel—the sadness and the glory of fixing to leave this world of struggle and pain for the better one a-coming.

> *"Swing Low, Sweet Chariot,—*
> *Coming for to carry me home;*
> *Swing Low, Sweet Chariot,—*
> *Coming for to carry me home.*
> *I looked over Jordan and what did I see,—*
> *Coming for to carry me home?*
> *A band of angels coming after me,*
> *Coming for to carry me home."*

Too soon the music ended, and while the applause was still sounding, I crossed my fingers and breathed in deep. The really important job of persuading folks that what they needed most was a genuine crystal ball reading was still ahead.

"Thank you all. Thank you all a whole lot," I told them. "Now if you'll give me another minute or so, I'd surely like to tell you all about what waits for you inside this very tent. Ladies and gentlemen . . . ladies and gentlemen . . . Want to know your future? Or escape your past? Let Princess Astrial, daughter of Victor, King of the Gypsies, uncover the deepest secrets of your heart. Princess

Astrial knows all . . . sees all . . . tells all. You will be enlightened! You will be amazed! Have a genuine crystal ball reading. One visit is worth a million words."

A man who looked like he'd just stepped out of an ad for Marlboro cigarettes called out, "How much does the Princess get for one of her readings?"

Could this be him, the rich sucker? By the assured tone of his voice, by his straight-on crafty look, and maybe most important of all by his fancy stitched real leather cowboy boots, I knew for a fact that this was no ordinary poor dirt farmer. This just had to be *him* that we had been waiting for all day. And now at last it was going to happen! Finally one of Mama's prophecies was going to come true.

"The Princess' prices are based on how much she can help you. Some folks she can help only a little and other folks she can help a whole lot. But wait a minute, sir," I said, lifting up a finger to indicate that it wouldn't take me longer than a shake of a dog's tail to find out. I poked my head through the tent's opening, signaling Mama with an elaborate roll of my eyes. Immediately she understood. So smacking her lips, she nodded her head yes, Yes, YES!

As soon as the rich sucker took his first step inside the tent, I began planning phase two: what all we're going to buy at the Piggly Wiggly Store. Hamburger, cheddar cheese, oranges, green beans, grits, okra, margarine, sweet corn, milk, one of those pork shoulders that they've been advertising, and two maybe three boxes of teething cookies and a Scooter Pie for Bubba Jay and Alice Faye who's going on seven.

Felt like Christmas in September! Finally getting some of the things we needed made me feel like I wanted to give away something to somebody else . . . at least a little something to everybody else. "Anybody here have any song requests?" I asked my audience. "Suddenly I feel like entertaining you all with songs that you want to hear."

An old woman with pale skin and wearing a straw hat that shaded her eyes from the powerful afternoon sun smiled cautiously, as though she wasn't much accustomed to getting something she wanted. "Do you know the song called 'Oklahoma'?" she asked before shyly admitting that she was born there in Oklahoma. In Lawton, Oklahoma.

"Uh, I'm not sure," I told her. "But if you can sing it, I can play it."

Then, without a moment's hesitation and in a voice surprisingly sweet, she began singing about her native state, "where the wind comes sweeping down the plains."

After "Oklahoma" somebody requested "Easter Bonnet," and when that suggestion was clapped upon, I made a request of my own. "Listen, folks, we're going to need some help here with the singing. So if I don't hear every one of your good, strong voices, then I'm going to send you all my meanest look. Right? Right! Okay, ready, set, GO!"

I felt so comfortable, so really happy being out here in the spotlight, that I knew that this wasn't the shy little me at all. This was Carlotta.

At first only a few folks actually began singing about the special joys of wearing a special bonnet on a special day. But all the while, in every way that I knew how, I tried getting some of those unmoving mouths a-moving. And miracle of miracles, before the song ended I did. At least most all of the women and even two or three of the men.

" 'When Irish Eyes Are Smiling,' " called out a man whose skin stretched tight over bones; but more than anything it was his eyes that caught me. Eyes that showed that they'd seen more than their share of tough times. Most people have to talk to a person before they know something about them, but not me. I read eyes. Sometimes I can be fooled, but still I know I can read eyes.

When I say things about a person's life, things that I feel are true without having what you'd call facts to back it up, people have called me down. Ask me what makes me so sure I'm right. But I just say, "Oh, it's just something I know." 'Cause if I told them that I know because I read eyes, they wouldn't believe me anyway.

For a while I was confused about how I could feel so confident about what I think I know and not at all confident about what Mama says she knows . . . all those past and present visions of hers that go parading through her crystal ball.

Finally I hit on the big difference: Mama sees things that aren't there. Maybe never were there. But me . . . me, I see things that are right there in front of me. All I have to do is just open my eyes and look in deep. It has a lot to do with being a Gypsy.

This is all especially hard for a gorgio to understand, but I know it has to do with how Gypsies are taught to look at things. Or, as Mama keeps reminding me, Gypsies learn to read faces long before they learn to read print. Almost no Gypsy *really* reads tea leaves, or even crystal balls.

Oh, that's what we pretend. But what we're really reading is faces. That's right, faces. In Mama's ball, for example, there's a set of mirrors that lets her watch the person's face as she appears to be gazing deeper and deeper into the ever-mysterious crystal ball.

Look, I'm the last person who ought to be saying things like that! Not any more than a magician ought to explain his tricks. After all, it's how a lot of us make our living.

" 'When Irish Eyes Are Smiling,' " I said, while adjusting the E string a half tone higher. "You can't be half Irish without knowing this one. My papa used to sing this a lot. Okay, everybody, on your mark . . . ready . . . set . . . SING!"

> *"When Irish eyes are smiling*
> *Sure it's like a morn in Spring. . . ."*

Together the voices were loud, joyful, and wonder of all wonders, on pitch. No question about it, we sounded pretty damn good. And every time I looked up from my guitar, more and more people seemed to be running over to join our singalong. There were a lot of familiar faces now: Tom Hackett; my last year's history teacher, Miss Dorothy Waters; Mr. and Mrs. Louis Leander Huntington, and Amber Huntington wearing a matching lavender skirt and sweater; the all-in-gray wife of Reverend Bartlett; and a good many other people that I grew up knowing.

> *"When Irish hearts are happy*
> *All the world seems bright and gay . . ."*

I only knew that I felt pretty warmed and wonderful myself. It was as though all those questions that I'm forever asking myself about who I am and whether or not I really have anything special to give were, at least for this moment, being answered in these singing voices.

> "*And when Irish eyes are smiling,*
> *Sure they steal your heart away.*"

Then suddenly a cry like an animal caught in a hunter's trap brought our singing to an uncertain stop. Who or what had cried out? Everybody was looking around.

"Let go of me, you stupid ass!"

Mother! It was my mother's voice! Suddenly she was shoved through the tent's opening by the rich sucker.

I raised my guitar like a weapon over my head. "Keep your filthy hands off my mother!"

Without obeying my order, he unzipped the jacket of his blue Windbreaker, exposing a bright silver star. "I'm Deputy Sheriff T. C. Anderson, and I'm taking this Gypsy into headquarters, where I'm booking her for larceny."

"Why are you picking on her? She didn't do anything to you!"

Wearing a sneer so deep that it looked as though it would be forever planted on his face, he turned to Mama. "While all the time claiming that she'd bless my wallet if only I'd place it on the table in front of her, she stole my money. Took out every bill I had! Now ain't that the truth, Gypsy?"

He must be lying. I don't think Mama steals other folks' hard-earned money anymore, not since she left Pat Patterson. Why, I made it clear to her from the very beginning that I didn't front for thieves. If I told her once,

I told her a dozen times: Reading fortunes is one thing, but blessing money is another. And she promised me that the only thing she's going to do now is tell fortunes—she promised me that!

Mama tickled his chin. "You're thinking that I'd go and do a naughty thing like that to you? To such a fine, handsome fellow like you?" Then she allowed her body to ever so lightly touch up against his.

He took a step in the opposite direction. "Enough of that! Who do you think you're dealing with, anyway?"

"Ohh," said Mama, making that a really long word. "Are you really one of those?" she asked, placing her hand across her mouth with a kind of pretend embarrassment. "You're one of those fellows, are you, whose second choice is a woman?"

From the spellbound audience came snickers and twitters of laughter as the deputy's face seemed to change colors as easily as one of those fancy jukeboxes.

"Damn Gypsy! We'll see whose money you'll be blessing now!" the deputy said, quickly jerking my mother's arm upward as she screamed out in pain. "Come on with me before I give you what for!" he shouted as he pulled her through the crowd.

I ran after them. "Please, hey, please let her go! Please . . . please . . . tell me where you're taking her. You've got no right taking my mother!"

Then, when he wouldn't answer me, wouldn't do anything but kept pulling her along with him toward the highway, I grabbed the tail of his jacket.

The deputy twirled around, sending his hand tearing across my face. Pain as sharp as a hunter's knife raged through my nose and cheek, sending me off the ground and then down to meet it.

Lying there in a crumpled mass, I wrapped my hand around my face, tasted my own blood, and wondered if I could still remember what it was I learned in science class about the major components of blood. The major components of blood? What am I, crazy or something? How can I think more about something that I learned back in ninth-grade science class than this that's happening to us now?

I looked up in time to see the deputy push my mother into the black-and-white sheriff's car before revving his motor and tearing off down the highway with sirens a-screaming.

At first I thought I must be imagining things when I felt someone standing over me, but I wasn't. Problem was, to see more than the polished brown pumps and the beige stockings, I'd also have to be seen, bloodied lip, tearstained face, and all.

Then there was a light touch to my shoulder, but in spite of all the lightness, it felt really solid too, like something or someone you could lean on. At least for a little while. "Are you all right?" asked a woman whose voice sounded full of concern.

I wiped my face against the inside sleeve of my plaid flannel shirt. Then, without looking up, I answered, ". . . I guess so. Sure."

"He shouldn't have struck you like that." Her voice was very close, only inches above my head. "A big, overgrown man striking a young girl the way he did. Well, that's a pretty unchristian thing to do, I can tell you that!"

I still didn't feel ready to be seen, but I just had to see her, so I looked up right into the blue-gray eyes of the slender lady on bended knees and discovered that I knew her. I couldn't offhand remember her name, but I knew that she was the organist at the First Methodist Church. Her husband, I knew him too. He owned the hardware store.

"Well now, let's get a look at you," she said, helping me to my feet. "See if you're still in one piece."

Until I could count on my knees not to buckle, I held on to her arm.

"Feel shaky?"

"I think it's passing now," I said, wondering if admitting this meant that I had to let go of her arm. "Where do you think he took my mother? To the courthouse?"

"There's no place else he could've taken her but to the Dexter County Courthouse."

"Reckon I better take down the tent and put everything on the back of our truck before driving over to see what I can do to help Mama," I said, as much to myself as to her.

"I wish I knew how to advise you, but I don't have much experience with these things."

As she spoke, I checked out her eyes to see if there was maybe a touch of malice in them, but I couldn't find any. "That's okay," I told her, but it really wasn't okay. Fact is, I could have used some advice.

"I guess we should introduce ourselves," she said, holding out her hand. "My name is Jean McCaffrey, and before the trouble began, I was enjoying your music."

"Thanks. My name is Carol Ann Delaney, and I already know who you are, that you're the organist over at the Methodist church."

"That's right," she said, laughing. "And if you know anything else about me, then you also know that when it comes to music, I'm real stingy with my compliments."

"I guess real fine musicians have to be," I said, pulling up one stake while she pulled up another. Finally, when the tent lay like so much canvas upon the ground, she helped me with the folding. Frankly, I couldn't figure out why she was helping me. There wasn't a gorgio in my high school—or anywhere else in this town for that matter —who'd turn their hand for a Rom like me. That may sound like an exaggeration, but it's not. It's just the truth.

❦ ❦ ❦

THE DEXTER COUNTY COURTHOUSE is a double-story white building set smack-dab in the middle of a grassy square of green. The offices are all on the first floor, but as everybody in this town grows up knowing, it's the second floor that everybody gossips about, 'cause that's where all the prisoners are kept. I drove the truck around our town's square several times before my heart calmed down enough to actually turn and angle park in front of a sign reading: OFFICIAL BUSINESS ONLY.

I cut the engine before answering that sign right out loud: "If getting Mama out of the pokey isn't official business, then I reckon I don't know what is."

During the summers, when Pa puts the wheels back on the trailer and we go caravaning with other Rom families, the talk around the night campfire often turns to officials. Town officials, county officials, state officials, and even federal officials. Gypsies hate them all, and if you had heard what I've heard and seen what I've seen, then you'd understand why.

One summer up in the Ozark Mountains, for example, it seemed as though every time we found a good campsite, the sheriffs and their men would make us move on. And that wasn't even the worst of it. The lawmen often insisted on searching our trailers, which really meant breaking our dishes and plunging their knives deep into our feather quilts.

Sometimes they'd use as an excuse that they were looking for stolen goods, but we didn't believe that. Like Grandfather said, if we Gypsies stole even half as much as people say we do, then we'd have to do our traveling in those giant moving vans.

My head dropped against our truck's steering wheel while I tried to figure out what in this world I could do. What could I do or say that could get Mama out of that place?

It suddenly struck me that it shouldn't be me here at all. If I had the sense that God gave a chicken, I'd drive right on over to the trailer and throw a bucket of water on Pa. If that's what it would take to rouse him from his two-six-pack-a-day beer-inspired sleep.

Then I'd throw the truck keys at him and say, "She's

your wife and this is your family. You're the man of the family, not me. So can't you for just once in your life act like it?"

Would I really say something like that? As mean as all that? I don't know. After all, the way Pa turned out isn't altogether his fault. How's he supposed to know how the man of a family is supposed to behave when he spent his growing-up years in an orphanage down there in Corpus Christi, Texas?

A flash of red light reflected against the truck's windshield. I half turned to see the familiar red neon Whitman's Cafe sign flash on for the first time this evening. It was there in Whitman's (how many years ago?) that my cold-stone-sober pa had taken me for my first piece of egg custard pie. I remember that he had gone on the wagon after weeks of nonstop beer drinking, and he was deep into one of his I'm-sorry-I-haven't-been-better-to-you-in-my-lifetime moods. And as his eyes glistened with tears that he didn't even try to hold back, he told me how much he loved me. "And how much I want to make everything up to you while I'm still alive," he said.

"Pa," I said, "I don't ever want you to die."

His arm was wrapped tight around my waist as we slid onto wood stools in front of the cafe's long, marble counter. Then, pulling a paper napkin from one of those metal dispensers, he gave it to me, saying, "Blow your nose and wipe your eyes. I don't want you ever to go wasting your good salt tears on the no-good likes of Painter Delaney."

He then said something that made me know that I loved him. I mean if I never completely loved him before or after, I knew for sure that I loved him then. "At least once," he had said in a hoarse whisper, "I'm going to give you something in your life that's sweet." That's when he called to the waitress at the far end of the counter, "Slice my daughter here a big, fat slab of your cherry pie."

But the cherry pie was all gone, and so for that matter was the apple and pecan, so that's why I had the only thing that was left: the egg custard. But that was good too.

🌱 🌱 🌱

IN AN ACTION that was so sudden it surprised the hell out of me, I pressed down on the truck's door handle and jumped out into the early evening air. Sometimes I do things like that. Move so quickly that my thoughts are so taken up with the action that I don't have time to be scared. And I've never, not in all my life, eaten a single chicken heart either, so that probably helps.

Short of starving (and maybe not even then), you couldn't get a Gypsy to eat a chicken heart. Not even if your life depended upon it! There aren't words enough to beg him or money enough to bribe him to eat even one heart of one chicken.

The reason is that the moment a chicken is grabbed for slaughter, all the fear rushes into its heart. Eat that heart and, the Gypsies will tell you, when you face danger, you'll be frightened, too.

I walked up the concrete steps of the graceful courthouse and into a large center lobby as though I knew exactly what I was doing. On the right were the now-shadowy courtroom and judge's chambers, and on the left was the only lighted office in the building. The black-lettered sign read: SHERIFF OF DEXTER COUNTY.

Because the door was already open, I walked in without so much as a knock. A young man wearing a uniform and a headset was talking into a standing mike. When he looked up, I already had my question ready. "Is my mother here? Her name is Mrs. Evangelina Delaney, although sometimes she's called Evelyn, too. Evelyn Delaney."

He took a couple of deliberate chews of his gum before answering. "That the Gypsy?"

Although I was angered by his question, I nodded.

"She was brought in an hour or so ago by Deputy Anderson."

"How do I get her out?"

"Pay her bail and she's all yours. She can be free on bail until her trial comes up."

"How much is that going to cost?"

"Fifty bucks."

"Fifty dollars!?" Fifty dollars . . . Fifty thousand million dollars. "Where in God's name can I get that kind of money?"

He took a ballpoint from behind his ear and scribbled something down on a memo pad before handing it back to me. "That's Ed Robbins' phone number. He's the only bail bondsman who lives right here in Bainesville. He could be down here in five or ten minutes at the outside."

🌷 🌷 🌷

THE ROBBINS PHONE was answered by a kid so young that it was clear that he hadn't been talking for very long. "Hi there, honey, could I talk to your daddy, please?"

Within moments another voice, this time a voice of authority said, "Hello, this is Ed Robbins."

"Yes, hello there, Mr. Robbins. I sure hope I didn't disturb you while you were eating your supper."

"It's okay."

"Did I bother you? I mean bothering a person while they're trying to eat their evening meal with a little peace and quiet is the last thing I'd want to do. If you know what I mean."

"Okay, who is this? And what can I do for you?"

In spite of myself, I sighed. No question about it. This is where the heavy work begins. "Well, you see, sir, I guess we're going to be needing one of your bails, or do you call them bail bonds?"

"What's your name?"

"Carol Ann Delaney, but the bail's not for me. It's for my mother."

"Who's she?"

"Mrs. Delaney. Mrs. Charles James Delaney."

"Charles Delaney? You all aren't from around Bainesville, are you?"

"Oh, yes sir, we've lived out near the Frazer place for almost twenty years. And my Papa used to work for the Department of Public Works until a few years ago, when he had to retire 'cause he couldn't work no more."

"Your dad Painter Delaney?"

"Yes sir," I told him. "Painter is his nickname. But Charles James—that's his Christian name."

"Look, I can't help you out. Already put up more money today than I have."

The phone clicked.

"Mr. Robbins, wait! Please . . ." For moments I stared at the silent black receiver that I held in my hand, knowing

34

as well as anybody that disconnected telephone connections don't ever just up and reconnect themselves. Not even the best Romany magic could accomplish that, so after moments of staring, I just put the receiver back on the hook.

I dropped my face into my waiting hands and suddenly cried out in pain. I had forgotten about the damage that Deputy Sheriff Anderson's strong right hand had done to my face. Gently my fingers began exploring the cheek, which was every bit as hot as it was swollen. And that's when it came to me that if it looked even half as bad as it felt, then maybe, just maybe, I had Mama's bail. My face would be her bail!

I walked right over to the young deputy, who was concentrating on blowing smoke rings. "I'd like to see the man in charge."

"That's Sheriff Long, but he's gone on home now. Won't be back till seven thirty tomorrow morning."

"Well, you'd better get him on the phone." I touched my right cheek with my hand. "Tell him there's a girl here who wants to report a case of police brutality."

Judging by the electric clock on the wall, only seventeen (at the most eighteen) minutes passed from the time I spoke of police brutality to the time that Sheriff Long stomped back into headquarters. "Come on back here into my office," he said, holding the door open for me, "where we can talk in private."

Leaning his large body back into his swivel chair, the sheriff aimed his half-lidded eyes directly at me. "Well, why don't you tell me exactly what happened. But first let me warn you of something, young lady, something you might not know. Deputy Anderson has been with this office for more than three years and we think mighty highly of him, so you'd better be right careful what you say."

"Yes sir, I will," I answered, already angry with myself for letting my eyes focus downward, remembering what Mama says about warding off "gorgio evil" with your eyes: "Look down or away and they think you're weak, but if you can keep your eyeballs fixed onto their eyeballs, then they know that you ain't scared of nothing."

The sheriff began scratching the back side of his head. "So like I explained it to you, girl, telling lies against an officer of this county is not just sinful, it's also about as illegal as you can get. Okay now, you got something to say, then say it!"

While keeping my eyes glued to his eyes, I pointed to the injured side of my face. "While I was pleading with Deputy Anderson not to hurt my mother, he turned around, and without a moment's warning he hit me hard. Struck me down in full view of a lot of people."

Suddenly the sheriff swung forward. "Other people saw this?"

"Oh, yes sir! Some people saw it and at least one of those people isn't one bit afraid to speak up and say so."

"Hold up now!" He held up his right palm in what I hoped was a sign of surrender. "Who is this person who you say is so anxious to report this . . . this incident?"

"The organist over at the First Methodist Church," I blurted out in a voice that I hoped sounded more confident than I felt. "Mrs. Jean McCaffrey."

I watched him smile for the first time. "Ah, Jean . . . fine woman. How inspiring it is to hear her play on Sunday mornings."

As he looked up her number in the county phone book,

I could tell by his winning expression that I must have really blown it. They see each other every Sunday, and even if they didn't, what made me think that a high-class gorgio like Jean McCaffrey would ever in her life take the side of a half-breed like me?

"Mrs. McCaffrey? . . . This is Sheriff Dan Long. . . . How you doing? Good, good. . . . I'm glad to hear it. Listen, there's a girl here in my office saying things about you that I know you wouldn't want said. . . . For one thing, she says that you saw my best deputy, Tom Anderson, strike her. . . . Wait, I don't think I heard you good. . . . You're saying that he did strike her? . . . Without provocation? . . . Without provocation. And you're sure of that? . . . Uh huh. . . . Well, as long as you say it, then that's good enough for me. . . . Only thing I'm ever interested in is seeing that justice is done."

Instinctively I knew that the time to push for Mama's release was the second he told her good-bye. "Sheriff Long, I surely don't want to cause you or even your deputy any trouble. Honest! So if you'll let Mama out of this place, I'll keep my mouth closed tighter than a clamshell. I mean about the police brutality and all."

Without uttering a single word, the Sheriff of Dexter County indicated by a quick jerk of his head that he wanted me to wait in the outer office.

I sat down on a chilly metal folding chair and told myself that whatever happened now, I sure did owe Mrs. McCaffrey a whole lot of thanks. Thing is I didn't have any real idea how much taking my side cost her. I wondered if folks hereabouts would think less of her for taking up an outsider's cause.

The wall clock over the young deputy's head read

six fifteen. I thought of Bubba Jay and Alice Faye waiting with pinched stomachs for me to come home and fix their supper. Why am I blaming myself? Always blaming myself. It's not my fault. I'm not guilty, not guilty, Not Guilty!

Quick, think of something else, something else, anything else. Counting the times per minute that the deputy chews his gum. Now counting and timing. Sixteen chews in fifteen seconds, or sixty-four chews per minute.

Lord knows I sure should have seen right off the bat that Mr. Anderson wasn't the rich sucker that Mama had been waiting for. If it weren't for me, she wouldn't be, at this very minute, caged up like some dumb animal. Gypsies can't stand—never could stand—anybody messing with their freedom. It's like trying to harness a lion to a plow. Stop it! Stopit! stopit, I'm not the mother. And all the responsibility's not mine!

After all, it wasn't me that went around prophesying that a rich sucker would come filling Ma's hands up with money. She was wrong as anything about that, but she sure hit the bull's-eye with the second part of the prophesy. The part that went like this: "Mark my words. This day will never fade from memory, Carol Ann. Not even when you yourself are an old lady and your mama here is resting with the angels will you ever forget this day."

New game: How many bobbles of the Adam's apple does the deputy's apple bobble per minute? The first fifteen seconds there were five definite bobbles, but the second fifteen seconds there were only two.

Six twenty-three P.M. Why won't the time move? Relaxrelaxrelax. Pa is probably home now seeing to the kids' supper. Six twenty-three. Still six twenty-three. What am I waiting for? I wish I knew.

Six twenty-three. Leave the clock alone. It's not bothering me. But are the hands forever stuck at six twenty-three?

Six twenty-four. See, time moves. Shame on you. Shame on you, Carol Ann Delaney, for ever having any doubts. Now, there will be no more watching the clock. What's going to happen is going to happen. I felt another sudden spurt of anger for Pa for not being here, for never really being here when we need him.

Closing my eyes, I commanded myself to remember some of the good things about him. Some of the things that make me think I love him. In the sunlight, his hair glinting reddish gold. When most men his age would be grateful for even enough gray hair to cover the bald places, Pa has a head crowned by reddish gold.

And don't forget his singing. Listening to Pa sing is a little like being wrapped inside something warm and comforting. His jokes are like that, too. First you laugh, and then you think, hey, nothing could be that wrong, 'cause look, Look! I'm laughing.

In all fairness, there are both good things and some bad things I could say about him, but I guess it was Papa who best summed up the truth about himself. Not so long ago, he was sitting outside the trailer door in the cool of the early evening, and I came outside and sat down next to him on the old oil drum that for years had lain rusting on its side. For a while we just sat together in silence before Pa, for a reason I never understood, spoke. "Some men," he told me without looking up, "are good while others are mostly bad. But me, I'm not a good man or a bad man. Just a weak one."

❦ ❦ ❦

FOOTSTEPS. Footsteps hurriedly making their way down the iron stairs. And then bells. The lilting sound of miniature Indian bells tinkling in an octave so high that no soprano would try to follow. I jumped from my chair in time to see a sour-looking sheriff accompanied by my jubilant mother.

"Mama!"

With the slightest motion of her mouth, she threw me a kiss at the same moment the sheriff grabbed her upper arm with a lot more force than needed. "Now because I'm a nice guy, I'm letting you go. So you just consider yourself one damn lucky Gypsy. But I'm telling you plain and I'm telling you simple that if I ever catch you pulling your fortune-telling tricks in this county, your daughter here will come looking for you *under* the jail."

He really began to shout. "You just stay away from our honest people or they'll find you *under* the jail! Understand!?"

In spite of Mama being a bare five feet, her chin was thrust high enough to give the impression that she was match enough for any lawman. Silently I prayed to God for help, because without the few bucks Mama picked up fortune-telling, there was no way the family could get by.

Then her eyes made direct contact with the big man's eyes. "I'm not deaf," she told him in a voice of almost eerie calm. "And I *do* understand."

4

THE NEWLY BUILT Bainesville Regional High School sits on twenty acres of flat land on the west side of the highway. Generally speaking, the town kids walk or are dropped off by their parents, while the country kids are bused. Since I live pretty deep in the woods, by the time I reach the road where the bus passes, I'd much rather walk than wait. That's one thing that Mama always says about me: "You don't know the first thing about waiting. And that's the Irish in you!"

Mama is sure enough right about that. Patience is something that the Gypsies know more about than the Irish. Go somewhere, for example, with a Delaney and they can't hardly wait to get there, but with my kinfolks the Yergises it's different. They're just happy to be in motion.

I probably have way too much trouble trying to figure out where in this life I belonged. Was it with the Irish or the Gypsies? And was I a country girl because I lived in the woods, or was I a townie because I walked to school?

How you get to school could have a big effect on who your friends are. The truth is that the town kids never had much to do with the country kids, but I don't know why this bothered me, 'cause I didn't any more fit in with the countries than I did with the townies. Maybe it's not this way in other people's towns, but here in Bainesville they don't much like you if you're different. And, boy, is my family ever different!

But just the same, I'd always gone out of my way trying to be nice, trying to prove that "different" doesn't have to mean bad. Once when I was in the third grade and Hannah Crouthamel invited me to her birthday party, I thought for sure that finally I had succeeded. Well, maybe I succeeded with Hannah, but I sure didn't succeed with Hannah's mother. She took one look at me, asked me who I was, and when I told her my name, she said that my mother wanted me to run right home. "Right now!"

"Yes ma'am, thank you for telling me," I said as I turned, and with my heart pounding with fear I began to run. And as I ran, I pictured my oldest nightmare coming true. Pa already had the wheels back on the trailer and he was now hitching it up to the truck. Wait for me . . . wait for me. But Mama wasn't one bit thinking of me. She was excitedly telling Pa that by nightfall they'd be up in the Ozarks with the Gypsy caravan. I heard myself crying out, "Wait for me. . . . Oh, please wait for me. . . ."

By the time I half ran, half stumbled into the clearing, I saw what I had never expected to see. The trailer, still sitting as pretty as you please on its concrete blocks, and our truck in the shed. Even so, I didn't have it figured out until I stepped inside the trailer to ask, "What's wrong, Mama? Why did you tell Mrs. Crouthamel that I had to run right home?"

My mama didn't look particularly surprised as she shook her head no. "Wasn't me who wanted you to come running home," she answered. "It was me who wanted you to stay and eat ice cream and have fun."

Even after that, sometimes somebody would talk to me and I'd forget everything that I knew to be true. Sometimes I'd even get to thinking that maybe this time it would be different. This time somebody'd like me, really like me. But usually it didn't take too long before even I'd come to understand that no, they didn't really like me. They just wanted to ask questions so as to satisfy their curiosity about us strange folks, us Gypsies.

The questions they'd ask me (and it didn't matter whether it was a student or even a teacher doing the asking) had a certain sameness about them. And I can't remember a time that I didn't resent them. "Do Gypsies *really* steal babies? Is there a Gypsy religion? How do you learn

4 3

fortune-telling?" And that question was almost always followed by this one: "Will you fortune-tell me?" And not always, but most of the time, they'd ask this question too: "Is there really a King of the Gypsies?"

I guess I gave the same answers so many times that they must have sounded memorized: "Gypsies are plenty fertile, so they don't *really* need anybody else's babies. Mostly we take up the religion of the country where we live. In Iran Gypsies are all Moslems; in Spain we're Catholic, and in England we're Protestants. On top of that—or I should say under that—we all share a Gypsy religion, too. So we have two religions—our old Gypsy religion and the new religion that we picked up on our travels.

"Now the question about the King of the Gypsies. Well, there really isn't one if you mean sitting up high on a throne and wearing a crown. But if you mean do the Gypsies have a leader, the answer is yes. Definitely yes. I'm proud to say that my grandfather, Victor Emanuel Yergis, was the King of the Gypsies."

Just because he was the King until he died three years ago, that doesn't mean that I longed to be treated royally. Good Lord, I'd have settled for being treated decently. In my graduating class, for example, there were seventy-three of us, and I betcha dollars to donuts that I could tell you practically everybody's name, but I'd hate to tell you how few knew that at birth I was christened Carol Ann and not "Gyp," and especially not "Little Gyp."

My teachers, though, would never in a million years ever call me those insulting names. Mostly they didn't really call me anything. If they wanted me to answer a question, they'd just point a finger directly at me while saying, "You!"

44

Well, even if they never got around to learning my Christian name, someday my stage name will be sailing from their lips. From everybody's lips! I can hear it all now: "Bainesville, Arkansas, takes great pleasure in welcoming back its native daughter. Ladies and gentlemen, let's hear a thunderous round of applause for that great composing and singing star, Carlotta Dell. Miss Car-lotta Dell!"

❦ ❦ ❦

I STOOD on the school's steps and watched as a familiar powder-blue Cadillac Sedan de Ville drove slowly, almost ceremonially, up to the school's horseshoe-shaped driveway. Directly in front of the door it rolled to a stop. Then the girl on the passenger side leaned over and kissed the driver before jumping out.

A radiantly smiling and waving Amber Lee Huntington started up the steps like a movie star triumphantly greeting her public. Any second now she'll be passing by me. Should I speak? Is it proper for the lowest of her highness' subjects to speak to the royal princess? Do I have anything like the nerve needed to say hi?

Carol Ann couldn't, but Carlotta could! "Hey, Amber," I called out, hoping that she didn't hear what I had just heard—the sound of fear vibrating in my voice.

For a moment or more she paused before looking directly at me. "Well, hello there. Hey, listen, you want to do me a very big favor?"

My mind blurred with the honor that was coming my way. There was actually something that I could do for Amber Huntington? "Sure, you know I will, Amber."

First there was a smile and then a delicate trill of

4 5

laughter before she answered, "Then you go tell your mother that I sure would dearly love it if she'd give my money one of her very best blessings."

I listened to Amber's laughter trilling all the way up the concrete steps while I stood in silence. In a dark, dumb silence.

🌷 🌷 🌷

As soon as I walked into my homeroom, Mrs. Erdahl told me to go straight to the music room. "Miss Thompson is waiting to see you, pronto."

I skimmed across all the possible reasons that the bird lady could have for wanting to see me, but my mind kept drawing blanks. "Uh, did Miss Thompson say why?"

"Only thing she said was that she wanted to see you. Pronto."

I stayed just outside the door, barely in view, until the music teacher finished checking attendance. One look at Miss Thompson and you'd understand right off why the kids refer to her as the bird lady. Everything about her is so unbelievably dainty. Suggy Peters once had the entire class in a state of near hysteria when she whispered the rumor that Miss Thompson is so delicate that when her period comes, she uses Band-Aids instead of Kotex.

The teacher gently closed her attendance book and then with a pale index finger beckoned me.

"Yes ma'am," I answered, walking over.

"Charlene Butler is out today with the flu, and since you have such a fine voice, I was wondering if you'd open the seventh-period assembly by singing 'The Star-Spangled Banner.' "

46

"You want me to sing? By myself?"

A thin eyebrow arched. "Charlene does."

If Charlene Butler sings by herself, then she expects me to do the same thing. Do the same thing as one of the most popular girls at Bainesville Regional High School. Carol Ann Delaney was wondering how she could flee while Carlotta Dell was wondering if this might not mark the natural beginning of her singing career. "Oh, well, yes ma'am, I guess I could if you want me to."

But as each minute moved me closer to seventh period, I began kicking myself for ever saying yes. Carlotta Dell had no business talking out loud, making important decisions for me, leastways not while she was only a dream. But maybe she was more now than just a dream. Maybe she was a growing part of me.

Instead of going to fourth-period lunch, I went into the third-floor girls' rest room to stare at the dreary image that looked back at me from the washbasin mirror. My pink peasant blouse had been washed so many times that the color had taken on a kind of grayish hue, but the jeans weren't too bad, or at least they wouldn't be if they weren't riding a couple inches above my ankles.

If only I had known! Had some sort of advance warning! Oh yeah? What good would that have done? It's not as though I've got something at home that's better. It's stupid, damn stupid of me to think that I can fill in for the girl who next to Amber Huntington and Tracy Cutter is the best-dressed, prettiest, and most popular girl in this school.

So what am I going to do now, Miss Show-off, Miss Carlotta Dummy-Dum-Dell? First go directly to Miss

Thompson. Explain to her that she'll have to get somebody else because I can't possibly do what I said I would.

I imitated her thin voice, "And why not?" she'd ask while her hands met in a kind of prayerful pose.

I barely have courage enough to speak about it to myself, so I doubt if I'll ever live long enough to say it to a teacher. Come right out and say that I don't have the nerve to stand up in front of an audience, letting them see me like this. Instead I'll tell her that I don't feel so hot. Probably even coming down with something. A cold . . . a fever.

In spite of myself, I laughed aloud at my own flimsy excuses before I found the laughter giving way to something else. Anger mixed with shame. I was ashamed of me . . . ashamed of my Papa, who was never anything better than a part-time painter and a full-time drinker . . . ashamed of my mother, Evangelina Yergis Delaney, who didn't care much about anything except Pall Mall 100's, Schlitz, Hostess Twinkies, anything cooked with onions, tarot cards, spooky talk, crystal balls, palm reading, and every afternoon television soap opera known to mankind, especially including *As the World Turns*, *Edge of Night*, and *General Hospital*.

And then it came, an explosion of tears. Tears as unwelcome as they were uninvited.

What a stupid, dumb person I am! I don't know anything, less even than anything. Well, maybe one thing. I know I need desperately to be special, to be Carlotta Dell, the Queen of Country and Western Music, but I am nobody but Carol Ann Delaney and is that ever common! Just as common as dirt.

The rest room door swung open, and so I dropped my head low over the sink, turning on the cold-water faucet full blast. All I needed—the last thing I needed—was bystanders and onlookers.

"Hey, are you crying?" First I recognized the voice and then I recognized the perfume. I looked up so that my eyes could tell me what it was that my ears and nose already knew. "Hey, you really *are* crying!"

"So what's that to you, Amber Huntington? What in hell is that to you!"

"Well, you sure are snippy, now aren't you?"

"Guess maybe I am! Guess maybe I didn't like what you said about my mother this morning!" I watched her eyes grow large, as though she was suddenly seeing something bigger, or at least different from anything that she'd ever seen before. Suddenly it struck me that maybe, just maybe, that gave me some slight advantage. After all, I'm kind of experienced at having folks be "snippy" and worse toward me, toward all us Delaneys.

"Jeez, can't you take a little joke?" she asked, her own hazel eyes showing that fear is no joke.

"It was you cast the first stone this morning, remember? But what you threw at me turned out to be a boomerang. 'Cause lady, your daddy cheats like crazy, and that's no joke! The only time, for example, that the weights at his cotton gin are accurate is five minutes before the weights-and-measures man from the state house comes a-calling. There's hardly nobody in this town who doesn't know that!"

Suddenly Amber exhaled, and I knew that there was a truce coming. "Hey, listen, I'm really sorry I said what I did about your mother. So look, like if you won't say anything bad about my daddy, then I won't say anything bad about your mother. Okay?"

"Okay," I said.

Amber turned, and took several steps toward the door before turning around again to face me. "So is that why you were crying? What I said about your mother?"

"Wrong again," I told her. "You haven't seen the day you could make me cry."

She looked puzzled, as though I wasn't leveling with her, and for some reason I wanted her to know that I was. "I'm crying—I was crying because Charlene Butler is out sick and Miss Thompson asked me to fill in, to stand up in assembly and sing 'The Star-Spangled Banner.' "

"Well, why not?" asked Amber, sounding her usual assured self. "You sing good. I heard you at the fair."

"Oh yeah, but you don't understand the whole problem," I told her while looking down at clothes that could easily be called rags. "Nobody should be made to stand up before every student and teacher in this high school looking like this."

She gave small, thoughtful nods of agreement. "Well, you've got to remember one thing," she said. "Everybody at this school is really quite used to the way you look."

If Amber had said those words to make me feel better, then she'd missed her mark. "What do you mean by that?" I asked, at the same time sure as anything that I knew exactly what she meant by that.

"Ohh, you know," she answered, smiling a mysterious smile. "After all, you *do* wear the same worn-out clothes day in and day out."

"I wear the clothes I have."

Leisurely, Amber ran her fingers across the monogram ALH that had been so prettily embroidered in her bright pink sweater. "Oh yeah, well maybe," said Amber, as though she suspected that I was really a Rockefeller pretending to be Cinderella. "Anyway, I think we'd better figure out what to do about it."

Did she really say we? I swear to God it sounded an awful lot like she had said we. I nodded quietly, waiting to hear if the rest of Amber's words would deny what I thought I might have heard.

Just then Amber's face showed that she had just given birth to an idea. "Because of lunch period, nobody'll be in the sewing room. Let's go see what they have hanging up there."

"There's nothing there that's finished. Soon as a girl gets the last stitch in, she's already carting it home."

"Hmm, there's got to be something someplace. . . ."

"What about those costume racks behind the stage, Amber? Maybe there's something there I could . . . borrow."

Amber followed me into the silent auditorium, down the center aisle, and around to the back of the stage where racks were jammed up with sequiny gowns, feathers, fake furs, choir robes, and even a medieval set of armor made from aluminum foil.

"This is going to be a real challenge for me," said Amber, examining the German soldier's uniform which was onstage for only a minute or two in our school's production of *The Diary of Anne Frank*. "What I plan to do with my life is to be a famous fashion designer." She smiled enough to show her dimple. "That's what my mother would have been—probably would have been one of the world's best-known fashion designers, 'cepting she married Daddy.

"Daddy wouldn't hear about her being a designer, but he's all for it for me. Says if I give my mother just a ten-percent discount, then by the end of the first year he'd be thousands of dollars ahead. Isn't that a scream?"

"Yep," I answered with not much more enthusiasm than I felt. "A real scream." I didn't mean to be sarcastic, but sometimes it's hard being what you'd call sympathetic to the problems of the rich.

"I don't know if you noticed it or not," I told her, "but the fifth-period bell rang a minute or two ago. You're going to be late for class."

She lit her cigarette as though she had all the time in the world. "I'm not going, are you?"

"No, but I'm desperate. What's your excuse?"

"Oh, I'll get away with it. Besides, if I can turn you into an okay-looking singer then I will have proved to everybody that I'm going to be a famous designer someday, like Calvin Klein, but with a lot more flair."

Amber's words put me into a kind of double bind, because they made me want to say thanks for taking on such an impossible assignment, Amber. And almost at exactly the same moment I wanted to blurt out, No thanks and anyway, who asked you for your help, Amber Hunt-ington? One thing I don't want is getting my feelings hurt, and so no thanks 'cause I don't need any favors from you. But the problem was that I knew that I did.

"Here!" she said, suddenly whipping a silky blue blouse from its wire hanger to hold up against me. "Hey, want to know something? This isn't half bad. Goes kinda nice with your complexion."

A gray skirt with a slight flare and even a pair of too-tight ballet slippers were found to replace the worn-out, old sandals that I was wearing. "Well," I told her, "I guess I don't know how to thank you enough for helping me out."

"You think I'm through with you?" she asked, making that sound like an outrageous question. "Well, I'm not!" She headed right over to the backstage pay phone. "There's still your hair and makeup to do. Hair and makeup are very important, you know, to the total image."

"Oh, I know," I said, not at all sure what she had in mind. "I know they sure enough are."

"There are still some things that we'll need," she explained as she dropped a coin into the slot and began dialing. "I want your hair to look shiny, full-bodied, and really terrific. And for what we're going to need— Hello, Mother. . . . No, nothing's wrong. . . . No, Mrs. Richards isn't pestering me about that dumb library book that she says I lost. . . .

"That's what I'll tell you if you'll give me half a chance. . . . Well, like the thing is, I have this project—you might call it a total design project that'll really give me the chance to strut my stuff, and I was wondering if you'd bring some of the things I need? Or have Letty Sue walk down with it? . . . My blow drier with *all* the attachments, my coconut shampoo, and my deep-protein conditioner, and what else? Oh, yes, my complete Revlon Beauty Box. The one with the twelve different-colored eye shadows, lipstick, rouge, mascara. . . .

"Well, I guess I oughta know a design project when I

5 3

see one. . . . Okay, okay, you can hear it from the beginning, but just remember that I don't have much time."

I tapped Amber on the sleeve of her sweater. "Don't you go putting your mother to trouble on my account." But she went right on talking into the phone just as if I didn't exist.

"Well, you see, Painter and Gypsy Delaney have a daughter named Carol Ann, and she's my age, but not in any of my classes—she's the girl that played the guitar outside the fortune-telling tent. And Charlene Butler is home sick today and so she can't sing in front of seventh-period assembly today, but Carol Ann can. Now Carol Ann, being a Delaney and all, doesn't have the guts to face her audience looking the way she does. Besides, I figure it would be good training for a future designer, not to mention fun."

This time I tugged rather than merely tapped politely at her sleeve. "Your mother probably has a lot of really important things to do and I surely wouldn't want to put her to trouble on my account."

Amber went right on staring directly at the pay phone dial. "Now, mother, you ought to know better than to think that! I'm not *involved* with anybody. It's just that I think it's a real interesting project— Hey, like listen! Why don't you come on down here and help me? You won't even have to miss your favorite soap operas either. Let the Betamax record them and you can play them back later on! . . . Oh, good! And bring the Polaroid so we can do before and after pictures. We'll show all the Huntingtons, and your side of the family, too, that Dorothy Huntington's daughter has got what it takes to become a really famous fashion designer!"

5 4

After Amber hung up, we dangled our feet over the apron of the stage and waited for the arrival of Mrs. Huntington. In the meanwhile Amber went on chattering about the time when she was only five and her folks discovered how truly talented and all she really was. Then she went on to talk about the advantages of being a leader in the fashion field. "One of the most interesting things is who you get to meet. Famous movie stars, presidents' wives and royalty, and a lot of people like that."

"Sounds like something you'd be real good at."

"Oh, I think so," she quickly agreed. "And if I can only make you look attractive, just think what I'd be able to do for the normal woman."

5

❦ ❦ ❦ WHEN LOUIS LEANDER Huntington's near-beautiful wife finally did burst into the auditorium, she was wearing a smile and a genuine fur coat. "Here's all the stuff you asked for, Amby," she said, raising up to eye level a canvas tote bag with the words "Nieman Marcus" written across the front in very fancy script. Then she turned toward me. "Well now, how do you like being a part of our little project?" she asked, lifting up a strand of my hair for closer examination.

"I'm not sure," I said, even though I knew it wasn't the total endorsement that she had expected.

"Split ends," Mrs. Huntington announced in the same serious tone that a doctor might use in telling a patient that the end was near. "But I thought to bring a scissors from home, and—and you don't mind if I cut your hair, do you?" Then she took out a camera and, without asking permission, she aimed it in my direction. Before I could think how I could explain that I didn't want my picture taken, the flash went off. She had taken my picture.

"Uh, no ma'am," I answered, knowing full well that if I had even half the courage that the granddaughter of the King of the Gypsies ought to, then I'd have come right out and told her yes. Yes, I do very much mind. But I didn't say anything, not a word. I guess it's only common sense that it's better to lose a little dignity in front of two people than it is to lose a lot of dignity in front of a full auditorium.

While I obediently shampooed my hair in the actresses' backstage dressing room, I got to thinking how nice this was. And the shampoo that carried an aroma of coconut made more white lather than I would have believed. But the whole time I washed, rinsed, and finally dried my hair with a towel monogrammed DHT, I heard the Huntington women arguing over whether "a layer or a block cut is right for her."

I asked them, "What's the difference?" since haircutting is something that not many Gypsy women ever have done, least not of their own free will. And if you ever see a married Gypsy woman with a shorn head, it's because her husband did it to punish her for adultery.

Because mother and daughter seemed much more interested in scoring debating points against each other than in answering my question, I repeated it while exaggerating each and every syllable. "I would like to know the difference between a layered cut and a block cut."

Immediately both women began describing with excited voices and gestures exactly what the cuts were and why one would look better on me than the other. All their talk and even their demonstrations on their own hair didn't, truth to tell, explain a whole lot. But it did, in a funny way, make everything better, because the explanations made them realize that there lived a real person inside their "little project."

"Well, I think . . ." I said, allowing the suspense to build. "That I'll go along with Mrs. Huntington's suggestion and get the layered cut." At least I had had my say!

They both worked on me nonstop until my hair was cut, curled, and finally sprayed with a can of Hair-Hold. Generally, it was Mrs. Huntington who concentrated on my hair while Amber (known to her mother only as Amby and, at least once, as Amby Pamby) filed, buffed, and polished my nails with a color called crimson sunset. And so I looked better, or so they told me, than I had ever looked "in all your born days."

Even so, it felt too early for me to become all worked up about the new me. And it wasn't as though I wasn't grateful, it was just that I wasn't what you'd call comfortable with it. Guess that shouldn't be so surprising, seeing as how I haven't as yet managed to get all that comfortable with the old me.

"All that needs doing now," said Mrs. Huntington, looking at me with a kind of owner's pride, "is getting the wrinkles out of your costume."

The girls' dressing room was equipped with a steam iron and an ironing board with a badly scorched cover that caused Dorothy Huntington to scowl. "How am I supposed to iron with this cruddy old board?" she asked no one in particular as she plugged in the iron. But right in the middle of her pressing my skirt, a broad smile appeared on her face. It was as though she had put something over on somebody, or maybe that somebody had put something over on her. "Here I am doing for you, Carol Ann, what I never ever have to do for myself."

She had called me by name. "Yes ma'am," I said, smiling back. "Reckon you sure enough are."

Suddenly a flash of light spilled across Mrs. Huntington. "Wait'll your bridge club sees this!" said Amber as she waited for the picture to roll mechanically from the Polaroid. "They'll never believe it! You ironing."

Dorothy Huntington patted her already-in-place hair even further into place. "You could have let me comb my hair first." Then she rolled the iron a few more times over the blouse before handing it to me. "All right, get into your singing duds."

Slowly I pulled the tail of my old peasant blouse from my jeans while frantically trying to figure how in creation I was going to get my blouse off and my new blouse on without exposing my bare breasts.

Back when I was in the seventh grade and the girls were

one by one beginning to wear those training bras, I asked Mama if she'd buy me one too, but she took it as a huge joke. "I was with the circus long enough to know folks who trained elephants, monkeys, bears, and even lions, but I don't think I've ever heard tell of anybody who could train their tits."

After that, I never really brought it up. So the years went by, five of them to be exact, and I never again asked.

Both mother and daughter were standing directly in front of me as Amber, showing more than a bit of impatience, said, "Well, come on now. We haven't got all day."

Nobody, I told myself, had ever died of acute shame. On the other hand, the way I felt this moment, I easily might be the first. Then, quicker than I believed possible, I slipped the peasant blouse over my head and in the next moments felt the warm blouse against my body.

I stepped out of my jeans into the flared gray skirt. "Tuck your shirt tail in," ordered Amber, and her mother carefully adjusted my collar. Then, stepping back together "to get an overview," they both stared at me as though I was one of their own prize heifers. What is it with them? Is that what being rich has done to them? Let them believe that only their feelings are fragile?

Mrs. Huntington once again brought the Polaroid up to her eye. "What an after picture this is going to make." She snapped and the flash went off. " 'Cause what we've accomplished here is nothing short of a miracle!"

For a couple of minutes the Huntington women talked between themselves about my before and after pictures before Amber held them out to me. "Hey, don't you want to see how much better you look?"

I took the pictures that I wasn't really sure I wanted to see. Would I look just horrible? Not just before, but after, too? The first thing that struck me about the two photos was that one girl looked poor and one girl looked rich. One girl looked like Carol Ann and the other like Carlotta Dell.

The seventh-period bell began ringing. Within a minute, less even than a minute, kids were going to be stampeding into this auditorium as though nuggets of gold were going to be thrown out. "Well, I guess this is it," I said to the Huntingtons. In spite of everything, I guess I'd have to be crazy not to be glad that they took an interest. 'Cause the truth was I didn't anymore feel bad about showing myself in public.

Then Dorothy Huntington went and did something that made me feel good inside where it doesn't show—or just maybe where it shows the most. She gave me a smile (a real person-to-person smile) followed by a wave from her perfectly manicured hand. "You look like a star, Carol Ann. You really and truly do," she said before disappearing on the other side of the curtain.

And then the auditorium door swung open and there was no doubt about it, the stampede was on. Frye boots, ankle-high work shoes, loafers with good-luck pennies in them, rubber-soled moccasins, and countless sneakers began pounding the hardwood floors with such impact that the huge room shook. It was as though deep beneath this town an earthquake was beginning.

But here on the private side of the curtain, I couldn't see the students in what sounded like a life-or-death struggle for seats. And what was even better, they couldn't see me. I know it was crazy, but I think I was falling in love with this moment, these few precious moments of privacy.

Then a slender hand parted the curtain barely wide enough for a bird lady to enter. "Carol Ann?" She stopped abruptly before placing a hand across her mouth. Probably to keep herself from screaming out in surprise. "Why, you know I didn't recognize you 'cause you look so pretty. Now don't you look pretty?"

There she had gone and asked one of those questions (or was it a question?) that I didn't rightly know how to answer. I mean if I say yes, doesn't that make me sound like the most conceited thing in Dexter County? And if I say no, no that isn't so (which it isn't), doesn't that mean that Miss Thompson's a liar? Or, at the very least, doesn't know what she's talking about? By the time I had an answer, she was more than a dozen steps away, standing by the ebony upright.

I walked over. "Thanks."

She looked puzzled. "What?"

"Oh, nothing," I said with a wave of my hand. "It doesn't much matter."

"What key would you like?"

I told her any alto key as Paul Collins brought the standing mike to stage center. "Testing . . . one . . . two . . . three . . . four. . . ."

Suddenly fear, like a deflected bullet, ricocheted through my stomach and I pressed my hands against the area of pain. Right off, I suspected that there was a name for what I was suffering. They call it stage fright.

I held both hands against my stomach and spoke silently but soothingly. "Calm down, now. You just calm yourself down, girl. Hear me a-talking to you, Carol Ann? Don't go calling me by that name, especially not now when I'll soon be standing before hundreds of sets of eyes.

"Sorry, sorry, let me try again: Those kids out there don't scare me 'cause I'm that great singer and composer known both far and wide. I'm the one and only Carlotta Dell! Now remember, Carlotta, that there's absolutely, positively nothing here worth being afraid of. You've never eaten a single chicken heart, so you're probably not really afraid at all. It just seems that way.

"Anyway, what's the worst, the very worst thing that can happen? They aren't exactly going to kill you, you know. No, maybe not, but they just might be able to kill my dream. The only one I've got."

The great room was quiet now. When did it get so quiet? Our principal, Mr. Simon Rudolph, known to everybody at school as Mr. Rude, strode purposefully up to the mike and then raised his hands like Jesus did when he was blessing the faithful. But before he spoke, he read from a piece of lined paper. "Teachers and students, would you all kindly rise while Carol Ann Delaney sings 'The Star-Spangled Banner.' "

And now I was here, standing here in the center of the stage, directly in front of the silver mike, looking over and across row upon row of faces. Were they friendly faces? How did I get here? Funny thing was, I didn't remember making the trip.

Then in the solemn stillness before the first note of the piano was struck, I heard a guy's voice carry across the width and depth of the auditorium. "LITTLE GYP, YOU WANT TO BLESS MY MONEY?!!"

6 3

An explosion of laughter was followed by even longer ripples of very knowing laughter that seemed to go on forever. I stood straight and unmoving while waiting for the voice within me, Carlotta's voice, to tell me what it was I must do. Soon enough the answer came: Let them play their games. They can't spook you, not now. Now that you're taking your first step on your journey to becoming Carlotta Dell.

As I looked across the vast assembly, I felt something happening. What was it? Mama would have explained it in fortune-telling terms. In low tones, she would have spoken about friendly spirits, long dead, moving into the body of the living to give courage when courage is needed.

I don't know if Mama's story is true, but I do know that something that had never happened to me before was happening to me now. I felt the power moving from the audience to the performer. Turning to my accompanist, I gave her the nod to begin.

"Oh, say can you see by the dawn's early light . . ."

Thank God for my voice. It didn't show even a speck of nervousness, and besides that it seemed to know exactly where it wanted to go and exactly what it wanted to do once it got there.

"What so proudly we hailed at the twilight's last gleaming? . . ."

And because my voice was doing real fine without any help from me, I focused on the words. Or more particularly

64

on what those words meant. Of belonging to a country that I was, in spite of everything, a part of.

"Gave proof thro' the night that our flag was still there.
Oh say does that star-spangled banner yet wave
O'er the land of the free and the home of the brave?"

The song had ended, and for a space of time nothing happened and then everything did. As though on signal, the faces of the students and teachers alike burst open, wide open into the warmest, most approving kind of smiles at the same time that they kept their hands wildly clapping. How could clapping get any louder than this?

And like before, there was a guy yelling something up to me, but this time I didn't mind, 'cause what he was yelling was "MORE! MORE! MORE!"

So finally I had done it. Won their approval. Never before and maybe never again after, but right now as I looked across row after row of cheering faces, I knew I had it and for now that was special enough.

❦ ❦ ❦ I f I h a d to use only one word to describe the difference in my life since one week ago today, when I sang "The Star-Spangled Banner," and now, I guess that word would have to be: visible.

Or to put it another way, all my life I've been almost invisible to almost everybody, and that's just as true for the teachers as it is for the students. But that's not true anymore. Teachers, for example, don't just point at me and say, "Answer"; they now point and say, "Carol Ann?" or in the case of Miss Thompson, "Would you kindly help the altos stay on key, Carol Ann?"

And town kids like Stewart Richardson, Pam Rodgers, and Barbara Cason—people who'd never even nod at me before—are now calling me by name. "Hi, Carol Ann . . . 'bye Carol Ann . . . see you around, Carol Ann." I heard them say that and I think maybe a miracle, as least one small miracle, has taken place.

On Tuesday Mrs. Huntington left a shopping bag brimful of clothes for me in my homeroom and said, "that had just been cluttering up Amber's closet." So I know I dress a lot better'n before. And Mama even promised me that when she gets her "new business going," we'll have money aplenty to get some of that coconut-smelling shampoo, the kind Amber uses.

Maybe after what happened when Mama made her last prediction, I shouldn't believe a thing she says, but she just seems so determined now, I guess I do believe her, at least a little.

I put my lunch tray down on the far end of a vacant table and wondered, with all the good things happening to me, when I'd get to spend my lunch period eating and laughing and joking with the others. At least today when I eat my spaghetti (one meatball) lunch alone, I'll have something wonderful to think about. That spectacular thing that happened to me since "The Star-Spangled Banner." I had my first date! And with Will Bellows. A nice fellow like that!

It really and truly was a date, and I'm only sorry that I went to the trouble of looking up the word "date" this morning in the largest dictionary in the school library. Definition 5b said: "An occasion . . . of social activity arranged in advance between two persons of the opposite sex."

I believe that those three words, "arranged in advance," make that an unfair definition and I've half a mind to write the Webster's dictionary people and tell them! Maybe if I explained it to them how it was with us, then they'd agree that what we had was a date, a genuine date. I'd start by telling them how I was walking home from school on Wednesday when I heard the tooty-toot-toot signal from a truck, and when I looked up there he was, Will Bellows asking me if I wanted a lift home.

Right off I was fair with him, and nobody can say that I wasn't. I told him that it would be way out of his way, 'cause we lived just south of the town line and the Bellows Dairy Farm is, as any fool can tell you, three or four miles north of the town line. But he just raised a chin that looked like it had been chiseled out of rock granite before smiling the biggest, best-natured smile that I had seen in a month of Sundays and said, "I don't mind if you don't."

Well, I no sooner slid onto the vinyl-covered seat next to him than he said, "Know something? You're one helluva singer. I mean it!"

I felt my face flush and I asked myself, is this possible? The girl who wowed the entire assembly is feeling embarrassed by a single compliment? Not possible? Yes possible, because the girl doing the singing knew that she was Carlotta Dell, but now with this fellow smiling at me, I only knew that I wanted to please him, but I couldn't 'cause Carol Ann was too shy to know how.

6 8

"Hey, you been yet to that new McDonald's they opened up on the highway going south?" he asked, but without waiting for my answer, he spoke again. "Every time you buy a Big Mac, they'll give you one of those little game cards, and if you're lucky"—he gave me a poke on my arm—"you could win a free trip to Disneyland."

"Wouldn't that be something?" I asked. "I'd probably have a heart attack and die on the spot if somebody told me I had won something as big as that."

"Wanna go?"

"Uh, well thanks, but uh . . . well, I'm a little short on money today and I might not have enough in my pockets for a Big Mac, but thanks anyway."

"My treat!" he said, while once again showing off his big, beautiful smile. "Won't cost you a thing."

"Well, okay, if you're sure you don't mind."

🌱 🌱 🌱

WHEN I OPENED the foam container, the smell of my first Big Mac told me that this was sure going to be some good eating. "I bought a double order of french fries," said Will, placing them between us. "So there's plenty there for the both of us."

While we ate (and I can't imagine any restaurant anywhere any better than this one), we just talked little talk, but as soon as our bellies were full, we talked about more important things.

"Both my mom and my pop want me to go away to the agricultural school in the state college over in Conway, but after Pete Tolen, I'm not so sure."

"Pete Tolen?"

"Oh, sure you know him. Blond kid. He graduated high school a few years back and went right off to Conway so he could be real up-to-the-minute about running his pop's farm. Well, Pete wasn't back any time before he had the place in bankruptcy."

"I don't think that would ever happen to you."

He looked surprised and pleased too. "You don't?"

"No, I think you're too smart for that."

"Yeah . . . ?"

"Yeah."

"Yeah, but you don't know me."

"I've known you a long time, and I know we've never really talked, but just the same, I've known you for a long time."

He looked puzzled, as though I had to know something he didn't. "We ever, like, had any classes together?"

"Miss Norsworthy's in the third grade, and two years ago Mrs. Berringer's history class, and once we went to the same birthday." At least for a little. "Remember Hannah Crouthamel's eighth birthday party?"

"Hey, you remember ten years ago? I can't remember ten years ago."

Because of Mrs. Crouthamel's words, it could have been a hundred years ago and I'd still remember, but I didn't want to talk about that. "Well, at the party, this fight broke out in the middle of Mr. Crouthamel's pigsty. . . ." I watched a slight glimmer of recognition come flickering across his face. " 'Cause Bobby McDonald and Owen Smith were making a game out of pulling suckling pigs away from their mother."

"Ohh, yeah . . ."

"You told them not to do it, but they weren't fixing to mind you and that's when the fight broke out. Everybody slinging mud pies and pushing each other down in the muddy goosh. Wasn't long before nobody could tell which were the pigs and which were the boys."

Will was chuckling now at the very same thing that he didn't find funny at the time. "If you think things were bad at Hannah's, right, then you should have followed me home. Ma took a brush to me for ruining my suit, and then when Pop came in from the barn, he took his hand to me 'cause I had gone and upset my mother."

Ten years after the fact, I felt sympathy for the young boy who had tried to save the piglets. "Hardly seems fair," I told him, remembering something I had read about double jeopardy. "In fact, I think it's positively illegal to punish a person twice for the same crime."

"If my mother heard you say something like that, then she'd go right ahead and make it triple jeopardy, honest to God. Hey, I bet you've got yourself a lot of those Gypsy guys chasing after you, right?"

"With my people, it's not like that."

"How come?"

"We don't go out with a lot of guys. Mostly our marriages are arranged by our fathers." Will was looking surprised, shocked was more like it, so I added, "We're really old-fashioned."

He was smiling like it was almost too good to believe. "You mean old fashioned in *every* way?"

I nodded yes. "We're supposed to be true to one man till death."

"Till death do you part," added Will while dropping a

71

deeply tanned hand on top of my hand and gently squeezing, and yet for all his gentleness, I felt his strength. Felt this strange sensation that I was being taken care of. . . . I hadn't felt this certain that everything was going to come out okay since I was little enough to believe that Mama could protect me with her Gypsy magic.

I sneaked a look up at his face. It was sure a nice-looking face, nice-enough-looking to be Irish. I wondered if he was Irish. Mostly, though, my eyes lingered along the line of his jaw. It was the kind of jaw that God reserves for Marine sergeants and football heroes. Yes sir, a man born with a jaw like that could absorb all the uppercuts that life could dish out. Absorb the blows, every single one of them, without ever once going down.

❦ ❦ ❦

FOR A TIME I stared down at my school's cafeteria plate, which was empty of everything excepting a cold, thin coat of orange-colored spaghetti sauce. And while balancing a spoon across my index finger, I wondered if it could be true that the only reason I was still eating my noonday meal alone was because I was selfish. I wanted everybody to do what Will did, come way on over to my side of the street. Maybe I just had to be more positive about myself, and not be so afraid to show people that I really did like them. Now that I'd sung, they'd like me too. Well, it was possible that they'd like me too!

What I had to do was to scientifically test out my theory. That beautiful theory that people really did like me. I looked across the width of the cafeteria in time to see Amber Huntington, Stewart Richardson, and Pam

Rodgers practically falling on the floor from shared laughter. Yes sir, before this very lunch period was over, I was going to be conducting a very scientific experiment of my very own!

But when I stood up to take action, I discovered that in spite of my strong talk, the muscles and bones of my knees had been replaced by so much jelly. I sat down again to search for just those comforting words that Carlotta could give me, words that could get me from this spot over there to Amber's spot.

What's so frightening, I asked myself, about being friendly to a friend? If she weren't a friend, would she and her mother have gone to all that trouble getting me ready for the assembly? And would Mrs. Huntington have brought me all those wonderful clothes? 'Cause going to trouble for people, isn't that what friendship is all about?

Again I stood up, and this time my knees seemed more or less steady. See, nothing to it. Now, walk yourself right on over there and say hello to your friend. Your good friend, Amber Lee Huntington.

Just as I reached their table, Amber gave Stewart a playful push. "Now, Stewie, are you or are you not going to get me another ice cream sandwich?"

"Not," he answered. "Definitely not!"

"Aww, Stewie, don't be such a bad ole meanie." Amber pouted, her lips pressed forward as though she was trying to imitate some movie star, but I'm not exactly sure which one.

Stewart grinned. "Well . . . say pretty please."

"Oh, prettyprettypretty . . . please."

"Now say, 'Stewie Richardson, you're the world's greatest.' "

Amber gave him a smile and a slight sideways glance. "The world's greatest what?"

He returned her smile with a private kind of smile of his own. "The world's greatest—you know. . . ."

"You're the world's greatest everything, Stewie. So will you please just go get me my ice cream sandwich?"

He stood up, and wearing the smile of the conqueror, he obediently walked off to stand at the tail end of the long ice cream line.

I moved even closer to take over the spot that Stewart had vacated. "Well, hello there, Amber," I said.

"Oh, hi."

"I sure have been wanting to talk to you, ever since you helped me out last week."

Amber looked as though she was more than mildly surprised that there existed, under the sun, some subject that might possibly hold interest for the two of us. "About what?"

Oh God! What am I doing here? Who told me to come butting in over here? It's too late to do anything but go on with it. I brushed some imaginary bread crumbs from my jeans. "I guess I . . . I just wanted to say thanks, show my appreciation."

She waved her hand like she was scattering birdseed. "Why don't you just forget about it; it wasn't important."

"Well, it was sure enough important to me," I told her. "And if it ain't too much trouble, I'd sure like you to come to my house on Saturday."

"Your house?" Amber repeated, looking first at me and then kind of knowingly at Pam Rodgers.

"Oh, I know you don't know the way, it being in the

7 4

woods and all, but I'd sure be glad to come by your house on Saturday morning and lead the way."

For moments she looked sort of amused, then uncertain, and finally determined. "Uhh, no, you don't have to do that. I'll meet you at Finn's drugstore at noon."

Pam Rodgers looked at Amber as though she had just up and taken leave of her senses. "Why are you going all the way over there? Over there to the Delaneys'?"

Amber allowed her eyes to fall softly on her friend. Then, without speaking a single word, she smiled a smile so sweet that at least for a moment I thought she must be smiling at some little new-born babe.

7

❧ ❧ ❧ I T W A S real hard concentrating on the political, economic, and social forces that brought Adolf Hitler to power. While Mr. Farrell droned on and on about the collapse of the Weimar Republic, inflation, unemployment of better than fifty percent of the people, the worthlessness of their currency, and the German people's long-

7 6

documented need for scapegoats and strong men, I could really only think about the wonderful things that were happening in my own life.

On Saturday, just three days from today, Amber Lee Huntington was going to be paying me a visit. Isn't it perfectly amazing what one "Star-Spangled Banner" can do?

When the last bell of the day rang, I slammed closed my notebook and began thinking about my outstanding debt. To let all these weeks pass by without so much as a thank-you-kindly is embarrassing. She was sure there when I needed her, no two ways about it.

Although the county telephone directory had given the McCaffrey address as 44 West Main Street, I discovered that not many houses on West Main Street (also true of East Main Street) were numbered. So I stood in the November chill in front of houses, cupping my ear like some kind of nut so I could listen for the sound of a piano. If the Sunday organist and weekday piano teacher had stopped the lesson to give a bit of explanation—or say that she taught her music from the back of the house—then I sure enough would be fooled.

Less than halfway down the block in front of a real nice white house with black shutters and a screened-in side porch, I heard music, if you want to call it that. A halting, many-mistaked version of "Beautiful Dreamer." Rest in peace, dear Stephen Foster, rest in peace.

Inside the screened porch were a couple of metal chairs and a white glider with fresh green cushions. I sat down on the middle cushion and began pushing myself back and forth while wondering if I was doing the right thing. Maybe she'd rather I just go on minding my own business without coming around here bothering her with my thanks.

I stood up, telling myself to beat it, beat it while I had the chance, when suddenly the door opened as Clyde Bullard, still zipping up his mackinaw, rushed through the porch and out onto the McCaffreys' gravel driveway.

Best as I could tell, Mrs. McCaffrey was first surprised and then pleased to see me again. And for the first time I guess I was really seeing her. Her face showed such honest good looks that I was reminded of one of those happy housewives who peer at you from ads in magazines like *Family Circle*. If a face like her face told you that one washing powder cleaned better than another, you couldn't hardly do nothing but believe her. Believe her even if in your heart you knew better.

"Nice seeing you again, Carol Ann," she said, opening the door wide enough for me to enter. "What a pleasant surprise."

And what a room for me to enter! You could park our whole trailer inside this one room and still have space left over. Except for a few touches of sky blue, the entire room was decorated in earth tones: beiges, browns, and splashes of autumn-leaf orange. In one corner there was a bookcase that was every bit as tall as me, taller maybe. And outside the school library, I know I've never before seen so many books in just one place.

"I don't want to waste any of your time," I told her as she pointed to a sofa with two matching lamps on either side. Imagine that! Having money enough to buy two lamps all in the same day. We both sat down on opposite ends of the sofa. "It's just that I've been wanting to come by and say thanks. You were sure enough a big help to Mama and me, telling Sheriff Long what you did. I know for a fact that he wouldn't have let her out of that jailhouse 'cepting for you."

"If I helped you all out, then I'm happy, too." She smiled. "Would you like a cup of tea? What I was about to do was to sit alone and sip tea, but it would be ever so much nicer if you'd join me."

I wasn't being pushy. She wanted me to join her. She really and truly did. "Well, if it wouldn't put you to any trouble."

Her kitchen was every bit as nice as her living room. There was this wood booth, similar to what they have there in Whitman's Cafe, where you can sit and eat and look out the window all at the same time. And Mrs. McCaffrey's linoleum was real nice, too. Looked like sand pebbles, and there weren't any worn places either. Well, maybe just one, over in front of the sink.

From the table I picked up a copy of *National Geographic*. "You do a lot of reading, don't you?"

Her mouth turned up into a smile, but her eyes didn't seem to go along with the gesture. "It keeps me company," she said, dropping three Red Rose teabags into a flowery china teapot and pouring in boiling water. We'll let it steep awhile. If you don't let tea steep properly, then you might as well be drinking hot water for all the taste you can get out of it."

"That's for sure," I answered, but I didn't really know that for a fact. The way Mama makes tea is to take a teabag, dipping it first in her cup, then in Pa's, and finally in mine. And by that time mine, at least, tastes mostly like that. Like hot water.

She placed the teapot on the table along with cups that

79

sat on their own matching saucers, teaspoons, white paper napkins, and a small plate of brown cookies before sliding in opposite me. "You know, Carol Ann, I'm so glad that I got to hear you sing at the fair. You're talented."

The words she spoke were words that she had spoken before, but I loved hearing them. Mrs. McCaffrey wasn't the first person to say that about me, either. My grandfather, Victor Yergis, had almost said that when I was twelve and he was only fifty-eight years old and already lying on his death bed.

At first the King of the Gypsies told me about the hardship caravaning used to be before most Gypsies traded in their covered wagons, called vardons, and horses for trailers and pickup trucks. "When the cold was bitter and the snow was deep," he told me, "we had to take all the blankets out of the vardons and throw them over the horses. But just the same those were good days, the best of days.

"And I was good to my horses all right, but that didn't mean I'd put up with a bad-tempered one. There hasn't been a horse yet born that could get the best of me. When a horse acted up, I'd give him a beating while all the time shaking pebbles in a tin bucket. After that all I had to do was to shake that bucket."

It was when he had finished that story that Victor grew quiet and I asked him if there was anything he wanted, anything I could get him. That's when he pointed to his genuine rosewood-and-ebony guitar and said it was mine. "You're the only one who can make it sing."

❧ ❧ ❧

I FELT Mrs. McCaffrey's eyes upon me as I stared down into the amber-colored tea. "I thank you for liking

80

my singing as much as you do," I told her, "but the best thing I do is compose."

Without bothering to mask her surprise, she asked, "You're a composer?"

Is she laughing at me? Thinking that that's an awful fancy ambition for such a common girl like me? At the same moment, I felt as though my emotions were being pulled in opposite directions. Should I confront her with my anger or convince her with my songs? "Guess you think that composing is a pretty weird thing for a girl like me?"

"I think composing is an unusual occupation for any-one. Would you show me one of your compositions?"

"They're not written down. I don't actually know how to read or write music yet. I only know how to play it."

I took the guitar that she offered while sliding out of the booth to perch on a high kitchen stool. Compared to Victor's guitar this was a kind of homely thing to look at, although the tone was nice. A little too soft for my taste, but all in all not half bad. After tuning, I let my fingers lose their stiffness by running through some chords. "I have songs for all occasions," I told her. "Songs to make you smile, songs to feel sad by, and after I read *The Diary of Anne Frank*, I wrote my first antiwar song. 'Don't Go Pigeonholing the Dove of Peace.' "

Her hands came together in a single clapping sound as though she could hardly wait for the show to begin. "I have a weakness for chocolate and anything else that makes people happy. So let's hear your smiling song!"

"Well, first maybe I ought to tell you that this song was inspired by a real, live event," I said, checking out her face to see if the connection between an actual happening and the creative use of that happening would be of any interest to her.

Best as I could tell she seemed real interested, so I just plowed ahead. "Remember, oh, a couple of years back when this crazy ex-boyfriend of the bird—of Miss Judith Thompson bothered her so much by acting crazy and standing her up all the time that she finally left him for good? I honestly don't know whether or not he went insane or exactly what happened, but I sort of imagined what her side of the story sounded like, and so here it is: 'Stood Up and Let Down,' words and music by Carlotta Dell—uh, that's me."

Accidentally using Carlotta's name like I did filled me with embarrassment. Up until this moment the fantasy known as Carlotta Dell had been mine alone. And yet truth was, Carlotta was becoming a lot more than a fantasy. Because more and more wasn't she becoming a larger and larger part of me?

At the same time that Mrs. McCaffrey was nodding, her eyes had narrowed as though she was focusing in on something that wasn't all that easy to see. I didn't exactly know what her look meant, only that my using Carlotta's name wasn't all that big a crime. And I think—I'm sure that it also meant that I shouldn't be so scared of my dreams because she was obviously a lady with a few of her own.

"*Waiting here on the old front porch*
Didn't you say you'd come at eight?
Honey babe, my lipstick's pale, my mascara's run,
Yet you swore you wouldn't miss our date!

"*The party dress and dancing shoes*
That I bought with you in mind
Are all worn out from all this pacing back and forth
You know, it's way past time!

"*Darling, oh darling*
Looks like our love is through,
'Cause here I am all stood up and
So . . . let down by you.

"*I rung your house at half past ten*
Your ma said you'd long been gone,
Then I called the pool room down at Sal's
But they just left me a-hanging on.

"*The picture show is closed tonight,*
Which leaves me wondering, too . . .
Are you up there on the Old Point Road
Holding tight to someone new?

"*Darling, oh darling*
Looks like our endless love is through,
'Cause here I am stood up and so let down by you.

"*I'm lying here, it's half past four*
And I can't fall asleep,
Every car that drives on by
I pray: let it be your jeep!

"*I'll never ask you where you've been*
Or how you've spent the night,

Just as long as you come running back
And make me feel just right.

"Darling, oh darling
Don't let our love be through,
'Cause it hurts . . . hurts way too much to be
All stood up and so let down by you. . . ."

Before the last note went echoing away, she rushed smiling from the booth to throw both arms around me. "You're something," she told me. "Really something."

Suddenly I was smiling, too, because Mrs. McCaffrey had gone and proved it. Proved what I already hoped was true, but didn't have any proof of until now, until right now at this very moment. She proved that I'm not one bit crazy or dumb, but I'm exactly what I thought I was. A singer-composer, pure and simple.

"Carol Ann, that song is a little gem! You mean to tell me that you haven't got that written down?"

"Like I told you, I don't know how to read or write music. But I have perfect pitch; Miss Thompson says I have perfect pitch."

"Well, you're going to learn! I'm going to teach you . . . if you want me to teach you."

"Oh, sure I do, but I can't pay for any lessons. Honestly, I don't have money enough for a single lesson."

"Don't worry about that! Worry about writing your songs down and applying for copyright. When songs aren't written, they can so easily be taken from you." She sighed and then her face softened. "And you know, I'd really like to see you hold on to what's yours."

Why is she being so good to me? Being a gorgio doesn't have to mean being an enemy, but just the same, I don't have any money for lessons, and so why . . . ?

"You look very deep in thought, Carol Ann."

". . . Guess maybe I am."

"Tell me about it, please."

"It's nothing."

"I'd really like to know."

". . . I've lived here in this town, not counting summers when we go caravaning, almost eighteen years, and so I was wondering . . ."

"What?"

"Wondering why when almost everybody in creation has a thing against us Gypsies, you . . . you're so good. Why are you? Why do you do it?"

She smiled as though she had been caught off guard, and yet she smiled as though she didn't really mind. "Oh, I don't know how good I am, since my reasons are decidedly selfish. For the sheer joy of teaching so gifted a student, I want to teach you. And something else. You don't have to be a Gypsy to know loneliness."

I nodded, but I didn't answer, at least not right away, because I was too busy wondering. Why was I born to one mother when I really should have been born to another?

❧ ❧ ❧ O N C E I W A S outside Mrs. McCaffrey's the air was cold as a witch's tits, but I felt fine because I was warm deep inside where cold can never reach. Wearing open-toed sandals and no socks, I began to run along the ice-glazed sidewalk. Running like an ancient marathoner. Running back to Athens to tell the citizens that the battle has been won and that Greece survives.

At the traffic light on Main, where the stores begin, workmen were beginning to string up the over-the-street Christmas lights. We're not more than a week into December yet and the storekeepers are already making like it's Christmas. Another thing I don't like is folks who go around pretending that this holiday is for kids; it's not. Leastways not for poor kids. One thing Carlotta Dell is going to do is to see to it that no Bainesville kid, no matter how poor, will be forgotten on Christmas day.

Past Whitman's Cafe, where the windows were so steamy that nobody could see in or out, I began to hit my stride. I flew across a small river created by a backed-up sewer, and discovered that in spite of the cold I felt just right. Look at me. Look at me! I'm a marathoner, the fastest runner in all of Greece and just possibly in Bainesville, county seat of Dexter County, Arkansas, too.

Look at me. Look at me. I'm Carlotta Dell all aglitter in a gown of sequins and feathers. Doesn't matter that I'm wearing a long and elegant dress and heels so high that my toes barely touch the ground, I'm running, running fast as I can. All the way to Nashville, Tennessee, U.S.A. . . . Running through the stage door and onto the floodlit stage of the Grand Ole Opry.

As soon as they catch their first glance of me, the entire one-million-member audience jumps to their feet while bursting into spontaneous applause. The exact noise level was roughly equal to a thousand locomotives, wrote the country and western music critic for *The New York Times*.

No need for me to feel nervous, I tell myself, 'cause they're all my friends, every single one of them. 'Cause haven't they each and every one been waiting for me for such a long time?

At the railroad tracks where Main Street spills into West Street, I saw that the Swede's—Mr. Cord Loggerman's—pearly pink Cadillac was angle parked directly in front of Loggerman's Liquor Mart. I thought that car was so ugly that it should, for all time, be banned from the road, by special decree of the President of the United States.

Kicking in its windshield and slashing its tires, oh, wouldn't I love to do that! Any fair-minded judge ought not to take any offense at what's my right. 'Cause how many of those dollars that went to buy that car were from our hard-to-get Delaney dollars?

At the end of the street, where West Street meets up with the highway, I ran south for about a mile until I reached the Frazer farm, where I jumped the gully and began catercornering my way through the field. A ways up, I heard the familiar gurgling of the Massoba River. Sometimes I like thinking about the river. Where it's going. Where it's been. And most of all, all those good, bad, and fascinating things that it must have learned along the way. Makes me feel good, as though I'm connected to something bigger, better, and brighter than just this place, just this Bainesville.

Pass the spot where the river bends and then look off to your left, and that's when you can see our place. For some people it would look like nothing more than a small aluminum house trailer in a clearing, beaten by time and weather. Well, some people can't see their noses in front of their faces, and that's the truth, too!

'Cause for all that time Pa gave up beer (almost seventeen months), he worked hard as anything on our home. That slanting wood roof built over the old flat tin roof was one big job, I can tell you! And an important one, too, 'cause before we had our new roof, the summer sun would strike the tin like a fire would strike a marshmallow.

When my grandfather, Sam Delaney, died in 1965, he willed my Pa this land with a house and a barn on it, and it was 160 acres of good, fertile farmland then. Now there's only three acres—2.8 acres to be exact—and I'm not real certain why Pa sold off his land, house, and barn.

Oh, I know it was for money, but that's not really much of an answer. Not when you stop to think that money goes, but land—land is something that lasts forever. At least it does if you don't go selling it off. And since Pa never farmed, but he did drink, I always sort of wondered if he used the farm money for beer money. No, I don't think he'd ever do a thing like that!

The trees around our trailer were all so cold and bare now that it was real hard to believe that only about a month ago we were all bringing our pallets under those trees every night to sleep. That way you could sleep on and on without having to fight for your share of the bed.

I think I'm pretty much over it now, but for years I'd feel a great sense of relief every time I'd get to just this spot where I could look into the clearing and see that our trailer was still there, still sitting there on its concrete blocks.

The fear first began one spring day when I was only in the second grade and poking along home from school. As always, my route took me past Loggerman's, and that day he was standing in front of his store, wearing what I thought at the time was a real friendly expression. "What are you moving along so slowly for?" asked the Swede.

"Don't you know your daddy's putting the wheels on the trailer today? And if you don't get home in one big hurry, your folks will be taking on off without you!"

"My mama and pa wouldn't do that!" I told him, but just the same I ran all the way home. At least until I reached that spot at the beginning of the clearing, where I could see for myself that our trailer was still there, still sitting undisturbed on its cement blocks.

But for some reason that I don't yet understand, I never (not then, not now) ever came out and asked Mama if someday she just might do that. Put the wheels on and move on off without me. Would she have laughed at me? Or just got mad and called me stupid, stupid for believing gorgio lies?

Just the same, for a long time after that, being deserted became my nightmare. My waking nightmare and my sleeping nightmare, too. Now that I think about it, I guess I'm only halfway over my fear of being abandoned. During the day when I'm at school, I don't worry about it at all, but every once in a while I still wake from that certain dream with a wildly beating heart.

And the memory of that dream is always the same: I'm running through downtown Bainesville, and as I run the sweat from my body is spraying some of this town's fanciest-dressed ladies. And because I've ruined their dresses with my sweat, they begin chasing me, shouting, "Little Gyp! LITTLE GYP!" as they run.

But it isn't until I reach the clearing that I remember how I had come to get myself bathed in sweat in the first place. I had to get home. My very life depended on my getting home before they hitched up the trailer and drove away, somewhere far, far away without me. But for all my running and all my sweating, I saw when I reached the clearing that I hadn't run fast enough, 'cause there wasn't a trailer there anymore. Nothing there excepting an old rusting oil drum and some cement blocks.

❧ ❧ ❧

FOR THE LAST FEW MINUTES of my run the cold had been too much for my thin-soled summer sandals, but that didn't matter anymore 'cause I was home now. All the same, I had just decided on the very first thing I was going to do when I became Carlotta. I was going to buy socks, one pair for every day in the week, and I'd even buy some winter shoes too, and just keep my summer shoes for the summertime.

Leaning up against the side of our trailer was the black-on-white sign that wind, weather, and time were coming close to erasing:

ONLY

THE GYPSY

Can Tell the Future
*
*Tea Leaves, Palms, Tarot,
and Crystal Ball*

As I pressed down the lever and pushed open the trailer's metal door, I was struck across the nose by the strong odor of pee. A bare-assed Bubba Jay sat on Mama's lap as she blew blue-gray cigarette smoke at the electronic image of three smartly dressed ladies in a Laundromat showing each other their dirty clothes.

Sliding off her lap, Bubba Jay toddled his T-shirt-covered body toward me. "Cowcowcow . . ." I picked him up, twirled him around, and gave his little behind a couple of affectionate pats. "Say Cah-ROLL, Bubba," I told him. "Now I know you can say Cah-ROLL, if you really want to."

"And just where have you been hiding since two fifteen?" asked Ma, turning away from all the laundry-minded women. "There's a lot of work here needing doing, and I'm not up to all of it."

I looked around. "Where's Alice Faye?"

"Out back behind the shed, watching your Pa slaughter the pig."

"The pig? What pig? Whose pig?"

She slapped her hands as though she was fixing to dance one of those fast-stepping czardas. "Didn't I tell you—weren't you paying attention when I told you that I was fixing to 'drab the bawlo'?"

"You poisoned a pig? Whose?"

She drew her pink chenille bathrobe close to her. "I didn't 'poison' it," said Mama, like she had no patience for stupid questions. "Nobody can eat what's been poisoned! All I did was suffocate it."

"How?"

"Know those pressed sponges I bought at Finn's? The kind that ain't got no more thickness to them than a postcard?"

I nodded yes while at the same time making a correction. "You didn't exactly *buy* them."

"Well, last night I took one of those sponges and dipped it into melted lard," she said, paying no attention to any correction of mine. "Then after it hardened, I fed it to ole man Frazer's fattest pig. Enough meat there on that porko to last us through the spring and maybe the summer, too."

I shook my head. "Once the sponge mixed with the pig's own saliva and stuff, it must've blown up like crazy. But I don't understand how you persuaded old Frazer to give you his dead pig."

Mama chuckled over the memory of her triumph. "I don't know if I'm going to tell you or not—you who stopped believing in your mama's magic."

"Come on and tell me, Mama, you know you're dying to tell me."

"Well, this morning, leastways it was before the seven-o'clock church bells, I went over to pay a call on that old man. Told him I had a vision last night he had a bad enemy who had gone and put a hex on him. First his livestock would die, one by one, and then finally he and the missus."

"Reckon you also got around to telling him that you are the only person who can shoo off the evil spirits?" When the good Lord passed out creativity, my mother came in for more'n her share. There's no question about that. "And you'd do it all for the small price of an already dead porko."

"And I did, too!" said Mama, who had the ability to believe in her own schemes so completely that sometimes I wondered just who was deceiving who. She licked her lips. "What I did was this: I took three dried and powdered toads' livers and lungs, chopped up real fine, over there to the Frazers'. Sprinkled the doorsteps (front and back), the barn, and finally sprinkled him and the missus, too."

Then her eyes closed and her body began swaying back and forth as she waved her slender arms over her head while chanting:

> *"Begone! Begone! Begone!*
> *To the Evil One . . . stay there!*
> *May thirty snakes devour thee,*
> *May thirty dogs tear thee,*
> *May thirty cocks swallow thee!*
> *So Begone! Begone! Begone!"*

I pumped her hand as hard as I safely could, but she didn't come out of her trance until she repeated her chant two more times. "Mama, I have something to tell you, too. Some good news!"

Finally her thin, sallow face came alive. "Really? Good news?"

"Well, I talked with Mrs. McCaffrey—you know, the lady that helped me get you out of the pokey." At the mention of Mrs. McCaffrey's name, I could tell that Mama's interest wasn't what you'd call high. "And you'll never guess what! Want to guess what?"

"If you want me to fortune-tell, then you must first cross my palm with silver."

"Well, I would," I told her, "excepting the only thing I have on me is gold. Anyway, I was fixing to tell you if you'd give me half a chance!"

"So do it," she said, glancing at the television long enough to satisfy herself that her soap opera hadn't yet started.

I didn't know where to begin, not exactly. "What it

has to do with is what I'm going to do. I mean my ambition."

"You'd better have your ambition all spelled out before this Sanka commercial is over, 'cause this is the episode where they're going to show Cynthia telling Doug that he's not the real father of their baby."

"Mama, things are going to happen just the way I planned it," I said, hearing the excitement rise in my own voice. "I'm going to write music and Mrs. McCaffrey—oh, Ma, she's a real musician, a fine musician—is going to teach me how. Won't be all that long before I'll be writing down all the music that I hear rushing through my head! And I'll make money, too. I'll be a star. Just the way I told you!"

Reckon it always surprises me that in spite of everything, this 115-pound body of mine every once in a while feels like it's stuffed plumb to the gills with confidence. Maybe it's not all that surprising when you think that early on we Gypsies are taught not to ever get hung up on what the non-Rom world thinks about us. So I guess I've already got years and years of experience in more or less shrugging off what my classmates think, say, and even do to me. After all, a good part of the pride of being a Gypsy is enduring what other folks can't.

Mama smiled, and I could see that she was already tasting the victory that someday would be ours. "WHOO-WHEE! Wouldn't that make their God-fearing little eyes come popping out! I warn you, Carol Ann, that the old hypocrites in this here town ain't going to be liking it if Gypsy and Painter Delaney's kid strikes it big. No sir, they ain't going to be liking it one bit."

"But we'd like it, Ma," I told her, looking into eyes so

black that it seemed one of nature's pure wonders that she was able to see out them at all. Maybe Mama really did, after all was said and done, believe in me. "Bet we'd like it an awful lot."

I DIDN'T KNOW if it was Alice Faye's arm or Bubba Jay's foot that woke me. Lying here like this, I could look up at the darkness, pretending that this here was a real house and what I was sleeping on was a real bed of my very own.

That's not all that ridiculous! When I really become Carlotta—I mean through and through Carlotta instead of just a little bit of her here and a little bit more of her there —then I'm going to help out my family. It's when I'm singing, composing, or studying with Mrs. McCaffrey that I feel like I'm every bit as good as anybody else. And what I can do, nobody can do better. That's when I know, for a fact, who I am. Know that I really am her, really am Carlotta.

One of the first things Carlotta's going to do is buy back Pa's 157 acres, house, and barn. Then Carlotta'll go to one of those big supermarkets on the highway and won't stop buying till she's spent a hundred dollars on groceries or maybe more. And Mama won't ever have to sell the trailer either just because they'll be living again in the house that once belonged to Sam and Olive Delaney. I'd want her to keep the trailer just for the summer when she likes to go off caravaning with our people.

And I don't one bit blame her for that. Some of the best times I've had in my life too have been traveling during June, July, and August with a band of Gypsies in campers, trailers, and wagons with incredibly high wheels. One family of six even owned a twenty-two-foot Winnebago. But you'd expect something fancy from those Roms, 'cause they had lots of money. Karl and Cindora, helped by their three sons, had the biggest driveway-paving business in Mayfield, Kentucky.

Some of the spots where we camped were so beautiful that when we moved on, I'd be tearful, thinking that we'd never again find anyplace this perfect. But to be honest, some of the places weren't good at all. Once, I remember, it rained every night for nine days, so the usual night meal with everybody eating, talking, singing, and telling stories around a blazing bonfire couldn't take place.

And lots of time the law comes by, and when they see we're Gypsies, they right away want to move us on over to somebody else's county. That's when some of the men will show off their gold jewelry and try to convince them that "We're not poor and we don't steal." Sometimes this works, and sometimes it doesn't!

The worst time was back a couple of years ago in the Great Smoky Mountains, when we had almost every one of our trucks and trailers sabotaged by some of the locals and, at the same time, the law told us that they didn't want us hanging around one minute longer than necessary. The sheriff himself carried a bullhorn in one hand and a rifle in the other. "And if you so much as look like you're going into a store," he told us, "then we'll throw the whole rotten bunch of you into jail."

While the men worked on the engines and waited for replacement parts to come from Knoxville, our food supply got down to almost nothing. For days we ate nothing but nettles, picked along the road and stewed in flour browned in goose fat along with some potatoes stolen by night and baked in embers. One night we kids raided a cucumber patch, and sprinkled with a little salt and pepper, those cukes sure tasted good.

Because every woman in the caravan tends to treat all the children as if they're her own, it took me a lot of summers to realize that not a single woman there wanted me to marry up with one of her sons. There were at least four reasons for that, and knowing what I do about us Gypsies and our beliefs, I have them ranked in my own head in order of importance.

One: I'm pretty sure that the biggest reason is because I'm a half-breed. My blood has been contaminated by gorgio blood. But Mama has a different feeling about that. As far as I can tell, Mama thinks that straddling both worlds is not altogether a bad thing.

Two: The women believe that I'll bring few, if any, children into the world. And no male children. It has to do with the way I'm built: a narrow waist and not at all what you'd call a fat ass.

Three: Actually, I'm not certain whether this should be ranked number two and number two dropped to third place: My folks have no gold, no money that I can take with me as a dowry when I marry. Now, to the outsider all Gypsies look poor, but looks can fool. All her life Mama wore gold around her neck, dangling from her ears, and flashing from her fingers, but when Pat Patterson dropped her by the highway, he took with him all of Mama's jewelry. Guess he wanted something to remember her by.

Four: I don't too much fit the Gypsy standard of beauty. The women, for example, are forever trying to get me to eat. "You got to put a little meat on your bones."

So I guess that's about it: the four reasons why I'll never fully fit into the world of the Rom. But there are at least four good reasons, especially since "The Star-Spangled Banner," to believe that I'm going to fit into the world of the non-Rom after all. Number one has got to be Mrs. McCaffrey and the way she's taking me under her wing. Funny thing is, if my singing that day hadn't gone so well, I don't think I'd ever have had the courage to go calling on her, either. Not even to say thanks.

Two: My friend, Amber Lee Huntington.

Three: My date with Will Bellows.

Four: The closer I get to really becoming Carlotta

Dell, the more I'm certain the gorgio world will take me in, take me in as one of their own.

No longer being a Gypsy. Hey, that wouldn't be all that hard to take! Living the life of a gorgio. People talking nice to me, calling me by name. And living in a real house. Amber Huntington was born into a great house, and I'd heard tell that she slept in a big bed that was meant for just her alone. Although I hadn't, in actual truth, seen her house from anyplace but the outside, I could sure enough imagine it all right. Reckon I'd spent a good piece of time imagining what it must be like there inside Amber's big, red-brick house. I'd also spent more than a little time wondering what the world must look like viewed from inside Amber Huntington.

I guess the thing is I wanted to know what it really felt like, being born special. What would it be like being Mr. Louis Leander Huntington's firstborn? Even so, there's no question but that we had something in common, Amber and I. We were the most different seventeen-year-olds in this town, but for entirely opposite reasons.

Once, I heard, when Amber was still a baby in her crib, Mr. Huntington came home with a hundred-dollar gold Bulova wristwatch for her to wear because he thought that she just might enjoy the ticking.

Special, she was born special, and I—I was born common. Common as field dirt. But with my talent, I just know I can push myself over that line and become special, too. And when I do, I want to take my family with me. Just the same, it's going to take all the talent and luck that I have for me to become what Miss Amber Lee Huntington already is.

A cry from a lonesome coyote startled the night and I

felt alone. Like the only person alive on a dark and desolate planet. In spite of myself I laughed. What could be nuttier than to lie so tightly sandwiched between my baby brother and kid sister that I couldn't move and still feel lonely?

Anyway, nobody is ever going to be able to tell me that being smack up against other bodies is a cure for loneliness. Maybe loneliness, or the lack of it, has more to do with touching feelings than with touching bodies.

I'm not talking from what you'd call experience, because the Gypsy code of what's proper behavior between two unmarried people of the opposite sex is very strict. Underline "very." Before a Gypsy girl is married, for example, she's not supposed to disgrace her father. And after she's married, she can barely look in the direction of another man or she'll have disgraced her husband.

Still, since my date I'd wondered things that, strictly speaking, I shouldn't ought to be wondering. Things like what would it really be like having Will Bellows lying here beside me? And if that was so, then maybe I'd never be lonely again. For one thing, we'd be so close I could tell him anything and everything. Make him understand exactly what it felt like to be me. Me, the daughter of the town drunk *and* the town crazy. But, no, I guess I couldn't any more say anything against my family than the man in the moon. They may not be all that much, but still that's all there is. All I've got.

🌷 🌷 🌷

WHEN THE BLACK NIGHT gradually turned blue and then bluish gray, I estimated the time at about six in the morning. I stretched my jaws and gave a silent yawn before crawling up and over the quilt to the foot of the bed.

For a while the sink water ran ice-cube cold, and then finally a bit of the warm stuff began pouring forth. That's when I slipped my flannel nightgown over my head while muttering to myself that no, no, I wouldn't die from the exposure. Leastways not today.

The house that Carlotta is going to own will have a bathroom big enough to hold not just a sink and a toilet, but a tub, too. Now wouldn't that be something! At the same time you're thawing out your bones in six inches of hot soapy water, you're also getting clean.

I rubbed myself dry with a towel that had long since become bald from overuse before slipping on a pair of jeans and a clean blue denim shirt that Pa had recently found lying on the gravely shoulder of the highway, not all that far from where he had found "his Evelyn" nineteen years before.

I brewed myself a cup of coffee and heated up a couple of leftover biscuits. There wasn't a speck of margarine around, so I "buttered" my biscuits with a generous slab of white lard. Although I could hear everybody's sleep sounds without really wanting to, this time, these few minutes, were still my time of the day. The only time when this little kitchen portion of the trailer was all mine.

The sugar bowl was scraped plumb clean of sugar. I think everybody would rather do without than go to the trouble of filling up that bowl. I reached high up onto the third shelf of the cupboard to refill it and saw three cans of beer left over from yesterday, which means that today will be only a two-six-pack day. Because Pa drinks about one beer every waking hour, that comes to about fifteen cans a day. So he alternates. One day he buys two six-packs and the next day three six-packs and so on and so on.

Used to be that every time I saw Pa's beer, I'd feel a fighting fury sweep over me, but that's not exactly true anymore. Now I can look at a can of the stuff and feel a lot more quiet sadness than violent rage. Besides, who's there to rage against? The beer? Mr. Cord Loggerman's whiskey store? Or Pa? My poor Pa. Somehow I don't much more blame Pa for drinking than I do Bubba Jay for wetting.

How could I? Seeing as how the drinking and the wetting comes from the same cause: not being what you'd call grown up. Maybe because Pa just don't rightly know how to be grown up and responsible. Oh, sometimes in bits and pieces he tries hard to be, but the truth is, he just never learned how. Maybe it's only because his own pa never lived long enough to teach him.

I threw a slab of freshly butchered bacon into the skillet before giving Alice Faye a couple of wake-up pats on the behind. "Hey, guess what I've got on the skillet, kiddo?" For a second her eyes blinked open before blinking closed. "Can't you smell it?" I asked. "It's your favorite thing to eat.''

This time her eyes and mouth opened at the same moment. "It's that fat old porko that Pa cut up."

"That's right, Alice Faye, and just as soon as you get yourself washed and dressed, I'll have it on the table for you."

"Okay, okay," she said, throwing the cover off both herself and Bubba Jay as she headed toward the bathroom.

As quickly as I could, I moved to re-cover our now-stirring baby. "Carol Ann's not going to let you get cold, babe," I told him while I felt the familiar urge sweep over me. It felt as though I was put on this earth to protect this child from everything from diaper rash and vitamin deficiency to his parents, who only seemed to be there. "If I could, Bubba, I'd take you away from this place. Maybe someday I will. To someplace that would be just our place. And nobody would ever know that you weren't mine, all mine."

❦ ❦ ❦ BY QUARTER TO EIGHT on that Saturday morning, Ma, Pa, and the kids had piled into the truck. The new shopping center in Wynne had the double advantage of being not only outside of Sheriff Dan Long's authority, but also a place where its citizens had never heard about the blessing of money.

At first both Ma and Pa gave me a hard time about my

refusal to come along. Although I told them (without mentioning Amber's visit) that I'd stay home and clean the trailer until it shined like the crystal ball, Mama only shrugged. "Ain't no use cleaning it. It'll just up and dirty itself all over again."

But my suggestion that Sheriff Long just might have alerted all the other Arkansas sheriffs to be on the lookout for a guitar-playing Gypsy girl and her fortune-telling mother seemed to go a long way in convincing them that maybe I'd better stay home today after all.

Earlier in the week I had washed (inside and out) every window; scrubbed every cabinet, wall, floor; and then washed and ironed all the curtains. So if I worked really fast, there was no reason why I couldn't have the place looking near perfect by, say, eleven thirty, when I'd leave to go meet Amber.

And when the hour of eleven thirty actually arrived, I wasn't disappointed. I don't believe that it's one bit of an exaggeration to say that the last time this old trailer looked so spic-and-span shiny was back in 1948 when it first rolled off the assembly line. No sir, today was one day that I didn't have to be ashamed!

"So much for my home," I said, giving myself a long, thoughtful look in the bathroom mirror. "Now, what can I do to make myself pass inspection?" I moved my face so close to my reflection that my breath fogged an almost perfect oval in the center of the chilly mirror. "Teeth are good, white and nicely shaped. Boy, am I lucky! I could have been born with teeth like spaghetti and I'd still never have gotten near one of those teeth-straightening dentists. Thanks for that, God." But just the same, I think it's my eyes, my black Gypsy eyes, that are my best feature.

Although my hair did look a lot better since the cut, I still wasn't happy with it. There was some flyaway dryness on the outer layer that reminded me of what I was going to buy when I came into some money. A bottle of that shampoo, the kind that Amber had me use, and never again would I allow laundry soap to touch my hair. Then I'd have what Gypsy women are supposed to be born having: hair so shiny that it looks like polished brick.

Back when I was in grammar school, I really did have a lot of shine in my hair, but not so much anymore. Not since the other kids laughed at me for doing what my Mama taught: wiping my greasy hands on my hair after I eat. It cleans the hands and, at the same time, it gives the hair a real nice gloss.

Searching through the medicine cabinet for a dab or two of hair oil to make my hair more alive-looking, I came across a large bottle of rubbing alcohol, a small bottle of Mercurochrome, a Vicks inhaler, a bottle of Heet and a jar of Vaseline, Pa's razor, and a box of the coarse salt that we use to rub on our teeth with our fingers. Does the same thing as a toothbrush and toothpaste.

I went back to the Vaseline. Oil is oil, I told myself, or in this case, grease is grease. Sticking three fingers into the thick, white glob, I began slapping it around in my hands to sort of break up the heavy consistency. Then I began to work the glob into my hair, but right off I had the feeling that this was never going to rank as one of my better ideas.

"Oh, damn! Damn! Damn! Looks like a damn grease cap!" And if that wasn't bad enough, it didn't smell all that terrific either. Won't take me more'n a minute, I thought, reaching for the laundry soap, to wash this stuff off, and then I'll run like the wind the two miles into town. I checked the kitchen clock: twenty minutes before noon.

Two miles in nineteen—or even eighteen—minutes shouldn't be any problem. One thing was sure, I absolutely, positively had to be inside Finn's drugstore at the stroke of noon. Not only is it rude to keep folks waiting, I wouldn't want Amber to think that maybe I had forgotten, and have her go wandering off with hurt feelings.

At exactly seventeen minutes before the hour, I squeezed water between my thumb and my finger and ran out the door. As I sailed across the frozen field, the water continued to drip down my shoulder and soon began soaking through my mackinaw. No matter how stingingly frosty my shoulders and back felt now, they were still in pretty good shape compared to my ears, which might, at any moment, come cracking off like branches during an ice storm.

Shouldn't have any trouble making it, not if I can keep up this run. If it takes me thirty minutes to walk it and twenty minutes to walk it medium fast, then surely seventeen minutes would be time aplenty to run it. "Well, just don't go getting too confident," I warned myself. " 'Cause this is absolutely no time for sprained ankles or broken legs."

Sprinting across the highway, I turned the corner onto West Street while trying to remember if there were any stores that featured clocks in their windows. Ben's Shoe Repair! Coming up on the right, the dusty window of Ben Serantides' featured a cardboard sign advertising Cat's Paw heels *and* an oversized clock. Five—no, more like six minutes before the hour. From this point, I could get down on my hands and knees and still make it to Finn's before noon!

Passing now a nicely painted storefront with the fresh gold letters on the windows, PARKER LEEDS, ESQ. *Attorney-at-Law*, started me wondering for the millionth time why all the people who point fingers at us Gypsies don't also take a few looks at the non-Gypsy gyps like Lawyer Leeds. Oh, I'm not trying to play innocent, 'cause I've borrowed vegetables from farmers' gardens and I've taken fruit from their trees and firewood from their fields; and truth is, I think Mama tilts too far toward greed what with some of the stuff she pulls, such as blessing money. But when I complain about it, she always says it's okay because we're in need.

Well, I for one don't think Mr. Leeds could even pretend to be in need. Every time Papa tells the story of his encounter with Mr. Leeds, his eyes mist up while his full lips turn into a thin, bitter line.

Pa starts his story in 1960. John Kennedy, the handsome young president, was speaking to his countrymen about courage, commitment, and new beginnings. And my Pa took his words so seriously that—that well, it was almost like a religious experience.

I mean his pride that "an Irishman like me" had scrambled to the presidency of the strongest nation in the world encouraged Papa to believe that "if Johnny can take charge of America, then I can at least take charge of Charlie Delaney."

So he gave up beer and took up working (and even working overtime) and saving money, and when Aaron Boyd's turkey farm, complete with 110 acres, 9,000 turkeys, and a five-room house with an attached barn, came up for sale, Pa understood at once that opportunity had come a-knocking. Knocking loud and clear.

And it would have been, too, if Lawyer Leeds hadn't seen Pa in town and begun giving him unasked-for advice. "I don't want you spending your hard-earned money to buy anybody's farm, Painter, unless you first have somebody you can trust. Somebody who'll look after your own interests."

Well, Pa's "hard-earned money" came to exactly four thousand, six hundred and eighty-five dollars (I used to know how many cents), while Lawyer Leed's professional advice came to a more rounded figure: five thousand bucks. So Pa had to give up his dream of buying Boyd's turkey farm and pay off Mr. Leeds instead. It was the law!

Directly in front of Finn's, I stumbled to an exhausted stop and leaned up against the lamp pole until my breath returned to something like normal. When, moments later, I did enter the store, I sure did appreciate the warmth. But even so the cold had seeped so far beneath my skin, deep into my very bones, that I knew I'd be cold for quite a spell.

Amber hadn't arrived yet because I was, according to the clock over the pharmacy department, still a good five minutes early. Just as well. Toward the back of the store where they sell cosmetics, there was a mirror that I could check out to see if there was anything that I could do about my looks in general and my hair in specific.

One look and I knew immediately what my hair reminded me of: a light brushing of frost on rather dry auburn hair. Even so, it was a better look than the Vaseline. What is it with me? Why is it that every time I get desperate, I just go and make matters worse?

I flicked the white frost from my still-wet hair (I should

have brought a comb) and then began patting it into shape. Just the same, it wasn't going to look all that bad. I hoped not bad enough to make Amber take notice.

There on the cosmetics counter were some sample bottles of spray perfume. From the one with the Frenchest-sounding name and the prettiest bottle, I pumped a couple of spritzes against my throat and then began remembering the springtime joy of lying down amid banks of wild flowers.

"Something you want to buy?"

I twirled around to whiteness. White cotton jacket worn by pharmacist Doc Finn, who dispenses every bit as much medical advice as any regular doctor.

"Sir? Oh, no sir, I was just looking."

He pointed toward the door. "Well, you go do your looking outside. This here is a store for folks who want to *buy* things."

As I walked like a sentry, back and forth, back and forth in front of Finn's and five other adjoining stores, I tried walking out, talking out my anger. No need to let my feelings against Doc Finn spoil the good times that I'm going to be having with Amber. Besides, how could he know that I'm not a thief? And if I had been more Carlotta and less Carol Ann, wouldn't I have told him a thing or two?

By quarter past twelve, when Amber still hadn't shown and I was wondering exactly when my bones had turned into ice glaciers, I knew that there wasn't a thing to do but to go get her. Probably she'd have wanted me to anyway, because she was in the middle of some small emergency. Maybe something very important that she had to do for her mother.

At the end of Main Street, Pleasant Avenue begins, but it's only in the second block that things get fancy. That's where Amber lives. I passed the Bainesville Community House, where a lady—Mrs. Hiram Cole—got out of her Chevy carrying a couple of aluminum pots. Some folks must be putting on the ole feedbag, and that's for sure.

The two groups that meet there regularly are the Lions Club for the men and the Missionary Society for the women. Now I know the Lions Club does good work, 'cause for three Christmas mornings running we've found one of their baskets tied with a red ribbon on our doorstep. And inside that basket were more good things to eat than anybody can imagine. Canned ham, frozen turkey, raspberry preserves, and even a pie-shaped slab of yellow cheese that came all the way from Vermont.

Amber Huntington's big, double-storied brick house was set back among evergreens of all shapes and sizes plus some real fruit-bearing pecan trees. Why, you could harvest enough pecans from any one of those trees to keep a dozen Delaneys in pecan pies.

As I walked up the quarry-stone steps, I came face to face with a front door that would give trouble to an invading army. On the right was the buzzer. I looked at it for what seemed like a long time before actually finding the courage to press it. Even then I had to ask myself what would Carlotta do. I heard what sounded like miniature church bells ringing throughout the house. Made me feel damn foolish, too. I mean all this activity just to announce to the mighty Huntingtons that Painter and Gypsy's near-frozen daughter was waiting to enter.

I heard the lock turn and then the door swung partway open. A black woman wearing a white uniform and a glad-to-see-you expression opened the door, and so I explained, "Hello, I'm Carol Ann. I have a twelve-o'clock date to meet Amber. Has she left yet?"

"Far as I can tell, she ain't as yet stirred from her bed," she said, bringing me into a hallway big enough to garage a trailer. "But if you wait right here, I'll go up and fetch her."

From the rear of the house a voice that I recognized as belonging to Dorothy Huntington called out, "Who's at the door, Letty Sue?"

"Just a girl for Miss Amber."

"Oh, all right," answered Mrs. Huntington, and I had the impression that she was disappointed that it wasn't someone for her.

And while I waited, I tried to remember everything. The standing clock that was a foot or two taller than me, a rug of such beauty that it must have taken a thousand weavers a thousand years to make, and a table of dark wood with feet carved like giant claws clutching balls.

First I heard mumbled words and then the soft shuffle of footsteps coming downstairs. And then I saw Amber wearing pink pajamas with dainty white lace decorating both the wrists and the Peter Pan collar. On her face was a look of near total amazement. "Well, what, pray tell, are you doing here?"

"We had a date, Amber! Don't you even remember? To meet at twelve o'clock today at Finn's."

"Ohh, no we didn't, 'cause I didn't tell you definitely. I remember specifically telling you that if I didn't have anything else that I had to do, then I'd try to stop by. But I didn't tell you *definitely*, so please stop saying that I did!"

"You did too!" I told her. "You sure as hell did!"

"Quiet!" said Amber, looking nervously up toward the head of the stairs. "Do you really have to go disturbing the whole house?"

I made my voice drop down, down to a menacing calm. "Frankly, I don't care if you come to my house or not, Amber. Either way it's okay with me," I told her, while at the same moment knowing that I did care. I cared an awful lot.

As her eyes seemed to grow larger so as to take in a new, more powerful me, I began to believe that nobody could get me down, not for long. Not me, not Carlotta Dell.

"Oh, well," she said, biting her tongue like a schoolgirl who has been caught copying from somebody else's paper. "Maybe I can go with you after all."

A few minutes later we walked outside into a December sun that seemed to be playing hide-and-seek among the clouds. I felt good about her coming with me, and at the same time I tried to forgive her. First of all, I had to get it into my head that she didn't really do anything all that bad. Why, forgetting a date isn't the end of the world. People do it all the time. It doesn't mean a thing.

When Amber and I crossed the highway to reach the frozen field, I warned her, "If you want to go the short way, you'll have to watch where you're walking, 'cause there's some patches with ice thin enough to step through. You can get yourself some pretty muddy shoes unless you're careful."

"Oh, these old things don't matter," she said, looking down at shiny penny loafers. "So let's go the short way."

But before the mud had risen much beyond her soles, Amber was already making noises like she minded aplenty.

"Guess you're not too much used to having your shoes get a little muddy?" I asked.

"Where I live," she answered without even a touch of a smile, "we have sidewalks."

I touched her elbow. "Want to see something?" I asked, leading her over to the high ridge beyond the river grasses. "Have you ever in your life seen a more beautiful view of the river?" I pointed. "Look over there to the right, where it coils its way downstream like a rattlesnake."

For moments she stared down river before lighting her exceptionally long cigarette with a gold lighter. Then she stared some more, and I came to understand that there's hardly anyone immune to the beauties of my river. Finally when she did speak, she was actually wearing a smile. "You oughta take your picnic lunches up here in the summer. It's so beautiful!"

"Sometimes I do," I said, feeling my good feelings for Amber beginning to return. "Sometimes I take a hunk of cheese, a little bread, an apple, and my guitar, and boy, I almost forget to come home. Someday I'm thinking I'm going to build a house, right up here on this spot. Damn thing is going to have so many windows that no matter what room I'm in, I'll always be able to see my river."

She laughed what I took to be a friendly laugh. "Sounds like you really mean business."

"Well, I guess maybe I do have a lot of feeling for this river. I've even written a couple of songs about it."

Amber's face looked skeptical, as though she wasn't going to let anybody put anything over on her. "You've written a song about a river?"

"Uh, yeah, sorta . . ."

"You're kidding."

116

"No, I'm not."

"Then let me hear it!"

"Okay, if you really want to."

"Go ahead."

"Okay, as soon as we get home."

"No, I want you to sing it now."

"My guitar's at home."

"I don't care about that. I want to hear you sing it here, by the river."

"I can't," I told her. "I need my guitar, and besides, my vocal cords are cold. I guess you think it's easy to sing when your vocal cords are cold?"

Amber sighed just the way teachers do when they have to deal with stupidity. "And I tell you that I want you to sing your river song here by the river."

I found G in my head, and then without saying another word I looked out over the swiftly moving waters and began to sing:

> *"Walking along the river,*
> *Walking along the shore,*
> *I find a calm that whispers, 'Go on*
> *Without my love.'*
> *Remember when together strolling,*
> *We promised love so freely flowing,*
> *Only I know now what I didn't know then,*
> *That rivers, like love, both ebb and flow.*
> *So I keep walking along this river,*
> *So I keep walking along this shore,*
> *Seeking the calm*
> *That helps me go on*
> *Without my love."*

11

❦ ❦ ❦ As Amber and I made our way through the field toward the single line of elms, I was real pleased to see that the sun seemed to have scared away the clouds. Because there's something about trailers that makes them look about a hundred times drearier than any other kind of place under steel-gray skies.

Once past the tree line, she pointed to our faded blue aluminum trailer set back in the clearing. "That's it?"

"Yep, that's it."

After a silence literally brimming over with thought, she asked, "Everybody live in it?"

"No, just the members of my family."

"What I meant was—"

I interrupted. "I guess I know what you meant."

"Well . . ." she said, turning that into a word crammed with meaning. "I sure didn't know that you were so touchy."

"What if I am?" I asked, looking at Amber out of the corner of my eye. "Guess maybe I've learned to be."

When I pressed down the handle and the door opened, I was suddenly impressed all over again by the unfamiliar spit-and-polish cleanliness and neatness of the place. "Come on in," I said, holding the door wide open for her.

For some moments she stood at the doorway as though she was glued to the spot, and it wasn't until I squeezed past her that I saw her eyes moving, right to left, left to right, back and forth like a Ping-Pong ball. Finally she turned her attention to me. "Everything's real handy here, isn't it?"

For me it was a new way of looking at life in a trailer. "Yes, I guess maybe it is."

Then, without much in the way of an invitation to do so, Amber Huntington began wandering through, front to back, asking about a quarter of a million questions on the way. "Who sleeps where? What do you all do when you have to go to the bathroom at the same time? Can you hear your daddy snore at night? What do your mother and daddy do when they *really* want to be alone?"

While I tried balancing my answers between not being rude and holding on to our privacy, I still felt as though I was somehow losing my clothes. The questions! When is she going to run out of questions? No clothes at all and still she pecks away. This is the sort of nakedness, like cold, that finds its way beneath skin to my very bones. Picking and tearing those last shreds of clothes and even beyond to the very marrow within my bones.

Still, maybe I'm like Amber suggested, "too touchy." If friends are really friends, shouldn't they be free to ask each other questions? Share information? Get to know each other? Sure, and if I knew more about friends and how they act, then I'd have already known that.

I watched Amber's face grow thoughtful as she tried to come up with still another question. "Do you think Painter and Gypsy will someday just decide to leave town and hook this old thing up and drive away?"

As sudden as a bullet, that old fear shot through me, and it took me moments before I could call that fear by its name: abandonment. "This trailer isn't resting on wheels! Anybody could see that!"

Also I felt uncomfortable about her calling my folks not just by their first names, but by those first names that the gorgios give them. Mostly I guess I was mad at myself for not having courage enough to ask her not to. Bet she'd do a double take if I just up and called her folks Louie and Dot.

And what she had said about my folks leaving, I reminded myself, didn't mean that they'd up and leave without me. Fact is, Pa puts the wheels back on every summer so we can go caravaning with the other Roms, but nobody has ever left anybody and nobody in this family ever will!

I pointed to our small Formica table with the now-shiny chrome legs. "Come sit down for a spell. I'll fix up something to drink. You like coffee, tea, or hot cocoa?"

"I'll take tea if you'll read my tea leaves."

"You have to have loose tea for that," I told her, although Mama had taught me how to make a buck reading fortunes in all sorts of ways: from the sludge at the bottom of Turkish coffee, beans thrown on a drum, tarot cards, crystal ball, and even by feeling for bumps on a person's head. "Ours comes in those little bags."

My new friend looked so disappointed that I almost suggested tearing away the bags and using the loose tea for a reading, but I didn't. The truth was, I was more interested in talking to her, getting to know more about her, than in performing for her.

Anyway, for a long time now I haven't held much to the view that the way those little tea leaves arrange themselves at the bottom of a cup could expose the past or reveal the future. Mama doesn't even believe in it when she does it for money, but just let her do it for herself and there's nothing she seems to believe in more.

Wasn't so very long ago that what Mama believed, I believed. One hundred and one percent! And just knowing that she had Gypsy power made me feel safe, 'cause there wasn't nothing or nobody that could harm me. Then, ever since I've been thirteen or so, I've been what you might call a half believer. But even that half belief had been pretty much blown away by Mama's "rich sucker" prediction that went backfiring.

Personally I think I could tell you more about a person's

character by the way they swirl their french fries into gobs of catsup or talk about their best friend when their best friend isn't around than by a mess of leaves at the bottom of a cup.

"Well, if you're not going to read my tea leaves," said Amber, "then sing me another one of those songs that you wrote."

"You want me to sing another one of my songs?" I repeated, just to make certain that I wasn't hearing only what I wanted to hear. I mean, at the time she sure enough did say that she liked "Walking Along the River," but how did I know that she was sincere? I mean before right now?

"I'll get my guitar," I told her, while deliberately turning my head away because I wouldn't want her to even suspect how important her compliment to me really was. My hands trembled slightly as I began to tune. "The song I'll play for you is something I'm working on now. It's called 'Wild Flower.' "

The first time I played the intro, I knew that I couldn't start singing, not just yet. Not until I felt myself Carlotta. So I played it a second time, and then I began:

> *"In a land where no one ever goes,*
> *Where water never flows,*
> *There grows a flower,*
> *One wild, wild flower.*
> *People ask,*
> *Can this be so?*
> *But only the flower,*
> *The wild, wild flower really knows.*
>   *Yes, it really knows.*

"In a desert where nomads never go
And oasis waters never flow,
There grows a flower,
One single wild, wild flower,
While wise men ponder,
Can this be so?
But only the flower,
The wild, wild flower really knows.
Yes, it really knows.

"In a home where no one ever goes
And nothing really grows,
Where light and laughter are truly sparse,
And love and honor merely games of farce,
There is a child, a lonely child
Crying . . . Oh God, oh God, keep me alive,
With your help I can survive.
So in this lifeless land of endless sand
I will grow into a wonderland,
Because I am that flower,
That wondrous, wild, wild flower,
And this flower really knows.
Yes, I really know."

As the last strains of the last chord began to echo off and away, Amber began to applaud. "Hey, that was kind of nice. Personally, if you want my opinion, I thought the music was a little slow, but I liked it okay anyway."

"I'm glad," I told her, thinking just how humiliating it would be if the opposite had been true. 'Cause if you feel something strongly enough then just putting the words and music together takes an act of courage, and then if you let somebody else hear it—well, that takes courage, too, and then some.

"Play another one of your songs."

I'd happily play for Amber all day and night if she really wanted me too, but right now I think I just want to savor this victory. Think about what it really means instead of just what I want it to mean. But it does seem to me that if she really liked "Wild Flower," then that would have to mean—wouldn't that have to mean that she likes me, too? "I'll play some more in a little while," I told her. "But right now let's have our tea."

"Can you find any of that loose fortune-telling tea?"

I laughed. "No, same tea bags as before."

Amber sighed, and I knew that someday soon I'd have to put my own feelings aside and give her what Mama calls "the deep soul" reading. The one that costs five bucks. "Oh well," she said, "in that case, I'll take the cocoa."

Reaching into the cabinet for the Nestlé's Hot Cocoa Mix (just add boiling water), I reminded myself that I have nothing in this world to be nervous about. For goodness' sakes, I can make hot cocoa as good as the next person. Haven't I for years been making it for the kids?

"And don't forget the marshmallow," she said.

"Marshmallow?" I repeated, feeling as though I was going down, down, down to defeat. "Gee, I didn't even know you liked them."

Her tongue made *tsk-tsk-tsk*ing sounds against the back of her teeth. "Have you ever in all your born days known anybody who didn't dearly love marshmallows?"

Just then, when I knew for sure that I was beyond help,

I had an idea! What I had squirreled away for myself would now save me from the terrible embarrassment of serving cocoa without a single marshmallow floating on top. I returned again to the kitchen cabinet. Only this time I reached way back to its hiding place at the very rear of the second shelf to pull out a half package of Hostess Twinkies.

I waved the prize. "You can have it."

"Never mind."

Reasoning that she probably felt real bad about eating the last Twinkie, I tried my best to reassure her. "I can't for the life of me eat but one Twinkie a week. Don't know why that's true," I said, talking as fast as I knew how, and at the same time unwrapping the see-through paper from around the not-quite-fresh yellow cake. I crumbled the paper wrap before placing the lone Twinkie directly in my guest's hand. "It's yours."

With slow and deliberate motions, Amber rose to her full standing height before throwing the oblong cake splattering, white sugary innards and all, against the shiny linoleum floor. "When I tell you *never mind*," she said in a voice that never once rose beyond conversational level, "I surely do mean *never mind*."

I saw what she did; I heard what she said, but I had to stare for long moments at that mess on my freshly waxed floor to really believe that it had happened. But still I didn't know why. "I reckon I just don't understand why you'd go and do a thing like that, Amber. 'Cause I just wanted to give you something. Be your friend."

With an elegant wave of her right hand, Amber announced, "That's silly."

"What's silly?"

"Ohh, you know...."

"No, I don't."

"Well," she said, waving her hand again, "it's just plumb silly to think that that could ever be true."

"You mean that you and I could be friends?"

"Yes," said Amber, looking positively relieved that it was me instead of her who had actually come out with it. "Why, I could never, not even in a thousand years, be *your* friend."

I felt as though I was now passing through a strange and frightening land. Too frightened to want to know more and even more frightened not to. "Well, why would— I mean, why for God's sake would you come all the way over here today if you didn't want to be friends?"

Amber smiled sweetly, as though she possessed some bit of information that made her just that much smarter than anybody else. "I suppose the real reason that I came over here," she said, pausing only long enough to brush some remaining Twinkie crumbs from her hand, "is to see your trailer. I only wanted to see if it was as filthy as people say."

12

By THE MIDDLE of May I had written the words and music to sixteen songs. Actually there had been a whole lot more'n that, but there were only sixteen that I liked well enough to call my songs. Some were funny and others were, frankly, sad; and if you pressed me about their themes, asking if there was one or many themes, then I'd have to admit the truth.

Tell you that I'm sorta limited, being that I only have one theme: L-O-V-E. Well, I'm not even so sure that that's true. Fact is, I also write pretty good about the absence of love.

What's really fascinating, at least to me, is that the songs that make people laugh and the songs that make people cry all have exactly the same theme. Then what's the difference? How they're handled. Some are handled in a funny way while others are given sad treatments. Now, having said all that, I still don't understand how it works. At least not in the intellectual way that Mrs. McCaffrey does. You see, mostly I work by instinct.

It's like my Thursday evening lesson, for example, when I was listening to Mrs. McCaffrey analyze my new song, "Chickenhearted . . . Lionhearted." As she explained in musical terms and technical phrases what was "terrific" about the song and what still needed working on, my instincts told me that she was right on target. What's more, I suddenly knew what I had to do to make the whole thing good, both the words and the music.

Anyway, I got so excited by not only seeing the problems but understanding the solution, too, that I began realizing all sorts of things. "It's really nice you helping me learn songwriting like you do," I blurted out. "But I can't understand why you're not doing it yourself. You know so much more than I do."

She smiled. "I know more, but you feel more."

"Is that bad?"

"Very bad . . . *and* very good."

"You're pulling my leg."

"Perhaps a little. As a composer, however, it's your

job to feel so you can bring your listeners into your world. Insist that we hear what you hear, feel what you feel.''

"Then that's good, isn't it? I mean isn't that good?"

"It's certainly necessary equipment. Beethoven and the Beatles had it in spades."

"So then what's the bad part?"

She shrugged. "Why don't you tell me?"

At this moment, though, I was only aware of feeling privileged, deeply privileged. 'Cause who would have thought it? Who would have ever believed that a real lady like Jean Bennett McCaffrey would have ever taken it into her head to like me? I swallowed back the tears that were about to rush into my eyes. She was looking at me waiting for her answer. But that was okay, 'cause I had one. "You get to experience everything. All the things that make you happy . . . and all the things that don't."

🌹 🌹 🌹

BECAUSE OF ALL the rain we'd been having, I couldn't take my usual shortcut across the deep-chocolate-colored fields. It was a real nuisance having to follow the longer gravely road, but just think what all this rain did to the farmers. They were already two weeks behind with their spring planting.

As I came near our lighted trailer, I heard Pa's near shout puncture the silent night. "Hold it, Evelyn! You hold on to that talk, woman, 'cause I've done a lot of things in this here world that I ain't proud of, but snatching bodies from the grave ain't one of them!"

"Now, now, Charles," said Mama in the same soft voice that she used for comforting Bubba Jay when he mashed his fingers. "I told you that you'd be having a hard time really hearing what I had to say. Now didn't I tell you that?"

From here, I could see Pa sitting at the table while Mama stood, leaning over him. "Nobody's asking you to steal nobody's dead body, Charles. All I'm asking is for you to *borrow* somebody's coffin." She reached out her hand to touch his shoulder. "There's a world of difference in that, don't you see?"

Pa shook his head. "Taking shelter from the dead . . ."

"But they don't anymore need it, don't you see that? We Gypsies have always known that! Only thing we ever use boxes for is carrying the body to the grave. After that we take the body that's all wrapped up in a white sack out of the casket and place it in the grave. The box we save to use again and again."

Pa shook his head like he was trying hard to shake away her words, but Mama only laughed. "You squeamish about that are you, Charles?"

"It couldn't be anymore unchristian than what you already told me."

"That's what you think, huh? Well, you weren't around when Jampai Jigmei, a Gypsy from Tibet, kicked the bucket."

"Can't say that I was."

"Him they gave a celestial burial."

"A what?!"

"Took him, or what remained of him, up to a rocky mountain ledge near Hardy, Arkansas. There they cut him up into bite size pieces and fed poor old Jampai to the vultures."

130

"Hey! You know I don't like that kind of Gypsy talk!" Then he slowly shook his head. "Why don't you let me build you a nice wood box to put the doll in?"

"Don't you *ever* let me hear you call Baby Belinda a doll! Not ever again!" There was a pause. A long-enough pause that allowed Mama's voice to change from rough to tender. "If we don't really believe in Baby Belinda, then how the hell are we going to get the suckers to believe in her? It's like Pat used to say: If you want people to believe in something that ain't real, then you always got to start off with something that is. A casket is something real. Something that people can put their belief into!"

Pa slapped his own cheek. "Ain't this the living, breathing end? Oh, Evelyn, ain't you something? Ain't you something else? Here you got yourself a display mannequin with a wig that you stole right out the window of the JCPenney store, and two dollars' worth of phony fingernails that you swiped from Walgreen's, and now you want me to dig up some long-ago-dead child's grave so as to *borrow* the poor thing's casket. Lord, woman, ain't there nothing in this world sacred to you?"

"Sacred to me!?" Ma's hand flew directly to her St. Sarah's medal. "Sacred to me—you're damn right! Eating three squares; buying a new dress before the old one rots off my back; and bringing toys home for the kids when it ain't even Christmas. Them's the things that's sacred to me, Charles. Them things and not some long-forgotten dead child's casket."

I heard Pa sigh as though the fight that was in him just wasn't in him anymore. "Let me get this straight, Evelyn. You really think you can have folks believing—"

"They're not paying out good money because they're all one-hundred percent believers," she said. "A lot of people will pay out good money just to have their curiosity satisfied."

"Okay, okay. So they're paying money to go into a darkened tent and—"

Again Mama interrupted. "Half-darkened tent, solemn like a cathedral at twilight. There'll be one lighted altar candle placed at the head of Baby Belinda's bier and another one at her feet. Incense will be burning and Carol Ann will be playing sad black spirituals on the guitar."

"And they'll cough up at least a buck, you think, to see Baby Belinda's long fingernails and hair?"

"They'll be paying because Baby Belinda died back in 1942 during the first year of her life. Killed in the arms of her mother, the beautiful Lady Pamela, during the German bombing of London. And for some reason, which is still a deep and dark mystery to all the most brilliant doctors in the world, Baby Belinda's fingernails and hair keep on growing at the rate of one quarter inch every year. It's truly the eighth great wonder of the world!"

"Sounds crazy enough that it might just work at that. Still . . ."

"Still what?"

"Only what I said before, woman." Pa's outstretched hand made him look as though he was begging. "Don't you think it's bad luck . . . might be bad luck mocking the dead? Respect for the dead, that's one thing I learned in the orphanage!"

"Like you said before, Charles, Baby Belinda ain't nothing but a doll. And we're not so much mocking the dead as we are poking fun at the living. Gorgios who'll pay out good money just to have their curiosity laid to rest. Now ain't that a scream!?"

"Maybe . . . I don't know. It just don't hardly seem right."

"I guess you think it was right what Lawyer Leeds did to you? Oh, don't you see, Charles, if only I had a fine child-size coffin, then we could do what magicians do for a living, make an illusion. Why, we'd have a real, growing family business that nobody, no sheriff or nobody else, could ever take away from us."

Pa laughed, but it didn't sound so much like a laugh as it did an expression of pain. "Haven't you learned yet, woman, that there ain't hardly nothing that somebody who's either a little smarter or a little richer can't take away from somebody else?"

Even after Ma and Pa had turned in for the night, I still hadn't gone into the trailer. Instead, I sat for a while longer on the old, rusting oildrum, trying to remember what we Catholics believe about our dead bodies. Back when Pa was on the wagon, we used to sometimes go to Mass over at St. Margaret's, but not so much anymore. So I don't know for sure. Do you need your body to stand in on Judgment Day? Pray for us now and at the time of our death . . . Jesus.

❦ ❦ ❦

THE DAY WAS breaking when I woke to the sound of our truck's doors slamming. At first I thought that Mama and Papa must be fixing to take off, but when I heard their voices, I figured that they must've just come home. "Ain't going to be half as hard getting this thing off the truck as it was getting it on."

"Boy, ain't it a beauty!" Mama's voice was full of excitement just as though it was Christmas day and she got everything she asked for and a little bit more. "Didn't I tell you I could pick it? Didn't I tell you I could pick a beauty, eh, Charlie boy?"

Then they went and did it, didn't they? I lay there with Bubba Jay's head resting on my arm, all the while trying to convince myself that there were other perfectly logical explanations besides the one that was now hammering against my brain. It would have to be something else because nobody, especially not believing Catholics, would ever do that. Would ever disturb the dead.

❀ ❀ ❀ E V E N W I T H my first step out the trailer door, there was no question about what I was seeing. From the back of the truck Ma was shoving a child-size casket down a ramp fashioned from two-by-fours into Pa's waiting arms.

Walking now toward my parents, I asked myself how

I could be so sure that I wasn't dreaming. I mean it was still possible wasn't it, that this was just another one of my realer-than-real dreams?

Using his shoulder as well as his hands, Pa gently eased the bronze casket onto the ground while wearing a grin that looked to me like it was touched with the pride of owner-ship. "Know something, Evelyn? Looks every bit as good in the daylight as it did in the moonlight."

At the first sight of me, Mama pointed to the coffin. "Looky, Carol Ann, looky here! Our own business. Sheriff Long can stop me from blessing money and fortune-telling if he wants to, but there's nothing on God's green earth he can do about the soon-to-be-opened Delaney Family Business!"

I stared at that thing until finally I broke my gaze to stare at Mama. "That doesn't look like a business to me."

She climbed down from the truck's rear platform to drop an arm around my shoulder. Time was when I loved it when she did that. Made me feel that everything was okay, that Mama would always make sure that everything was okay. But now I'm not so certain. "Well, that's sure enough what it is, Carol Ann, 'cause we're going to give the paying public something that's going to fire them right up. A glimpse of life after death . . . or at least of nails and hair that keep on growing after death."

Water, earth, and the ages had rusted out a band of bronze along the edges. What, I wondered, had those same natural elements done to the child that lay inside?

Mama was using her hands in that quick animated way that she does when she gets excited. "The way I see it, we've got to play this big. Give it the old razzamatazz same way Procter & Gamble does when they got themselves a new soap to sell."

I asked, "Anybody in there?"

"Oh, Lord no," said Mama as though she was horrified that I would, even for a moment, accuse her of such a thing. "We buried her back in the same spot, even said a prayer over her. It was real dignified—ain't that right, Charles?"

Pa's face was caught wearing a this-is-all-news-to-me look, but Mama went right on talking. "And we done it all in the natural Gypsy way. Earth mingling with bones, the way it should've been done in the first place."

"You shouldn't've done it," I told her.

"Why, I think we did a blessed thing. What with the prayers and all."

Pa's always-thin face suddenly looked as though he was under a great strain. "Don't go saying anything to anybody about this, Carol Ann. A lot of folks wouldn't understand."

Did Pa mean by that there were people who would understand? Then maybe one of them would be nice enough to explain it to me.

"Carol Ann, you hear me a-talking to you?"

"Yes sir," I answered. "I surely do."

"Advertising," said Mama, raising a single finger skyward. "That's the key to success! How else can you explain why folks pay out good money for bad-tasting soda? And you're thinking—I just bet you're thinking that those companies have money to buy advertising and soap companies got money to buy advertising with, but we Delaneys ain't got no advertising money.

"Well, the great Princess Astrial has all that figured out, too. First we pitch Baby Belinda's tent on places like the junction to the Wynne highway. And we'll put up signs, coming and going. Signs big enough to knock your eyeballs out. And all those signs are going to be advertising our own amazing Baby Belinda, the eighth great wonder of the modern world. So what do you think of your old ma now? Well, say something!"

"What's her name?"

"Baby Belinda," she said, pronouncing the name with great care. "I thought it up myself. Sounds so sweet and fancy and magical, don't you think so?"

"I mean," I said, pointing to the coffin, "the name of the child that lay in there?"

"Oh, that name," said Mama, looking disappointed that her creativity was going unappreciated. "Sarah Jones. She was born during the summer of 1915 and died in the winter —January, I think it was—of 1920."

"Sixty-two years," I said to no one in particular. "She's been lying there peaceably for sixty-two years."

"So that's it," said Mama, fixing her hands to her hips. "You and your Papa done come right out of the same bolt of cloth, didn't you? Him and you both worrying yourself sick about the already dead, now ain't that the truth?"

"I don't know," I said. "Maybe."

"Well, let me tell you something, young lady. I'm pure Gypsy and not no half-breed like you! And with every one of us one-hundred-percent pure Roms there's always something racing through our blood. It's right in the blood, if you ask me. Know what that is?" she asked, and without pausing to hear my answer, she gave her own. "A little voice that keeps crying out. Sometimes it cries softly and sometimes it screams, but no matter how it says it, the words are always the same: Survive. . . . Survive! . . . SURVIVE!"

"You don't have to shout, Mama. I'm not exactly deaf, you know."

"Yeah, well sometimes I wonder if you're not a little too touched in the heart with softness to survive, if you want my opinion. Once when you weren't much bigger than Bubba Jay is now, you came running to me, crying and carrying on at the top of your lungs. I thought for sure that you had gone and hurt yourself, but, no . . . that wasn't it at all. You saw a dead field mouse and you were crying for that mouse. Can you believe that? Crying and wailing yourself sick over a dead field mouse?"

"Yes, I guess I can," I told her. "Because I can remember it still. It's almost the first thing that I do remember."

"Then when you going to learn?" asked Mama, her black eyes flashing fire. "When you ever going to learn that if you're a Gypsy, then you belong to the most put-down, put-upon people on the face of this earth. No other folks even come close. And so you've always got to be fighting, fighting and tearing other people off your back, and that's why you can't be wasting good tears on dead mice or long-ago dead children."

"Your ma is talking good sense to you, girl, so perk up your ears and pay attention."

In a way that I had never before looked at her, I looked at her now. What I saw was that in spite of the long flowered skirt that went bouncing around her ankles, she wore the pants in this family. Then I looked at Pa and I could just tell that his blood was tired and thin. And it had been a long time (maybe not since John Kennedy) that there had been any voices within him crying out for survival. If Pa cried out for anything these days, it would, more than likely, be for a beer. But then it just may be that for Papa, beer was survival.

Suddenly my forearms were being gripped in Pa's vise-like hands. "When I'm a-talking to you, girl, I expect to hear an answer."

"I don't know what you want me to say."

He looked off in the distance as though the answer to my question was somewhere out there, just beyond his reach. "Well," he said, releasing his grip. "Start off by taking that look off your face."

Ma nodded her agreement. "Your pa's right. You look like you is going around with your nose stuck up high and mighty, like you and that music teacher of yours is too good to be breathing in the same air as your pa and me."

"I never said that!" I said, at the same time asking myself if I didn't think it.

"You never had to," said Ma. "You're all the time talking about your highfalutin ideas. Being a singing star and a composer, too. Well, if you want my opinion," said Ma, smiling sweetly and then bowing low as though greeting royalty, "my lowly, low opinion is that composing is meant for fancy gorgios and not for none of us Delaneys."

"That's not true!" I told her while feeling that just maybe it was. And maybe her words also accomplished something else: Maybe they were pushing my fragile dreams away.

"Oh, it's true enough." Her face held on to that smile, that Gypsy smile that says that she, after all, knows what's going to be while dumb ole me hasn't even got around to figuring out what already has been. " 'Cause I read it in the tarot, and I read the very same message in the ball."

I didn't want Mama to know that her words were affecting me, so I looked right up at her, but she went right on talking. "What I asked the cards and the ball was this: Tell me where this lust for fame and fortune is going to lead our Carol Ann."

"And what was their answer?"

She stared at me for what seemed like an endless moment before taking hold of my left hand and turning it palm side up. "There's no special gifts hiding in this hand." She brushed my hand clean of imaginary dust. "Oh, the lines show some determination, but talent?" She laughed at the word "talent." "There's none of that in this hand, and if you go running after this crazy dream of yours, it won't lead you onto no shining boulevards of fame and riches. Oh, no, the journey will take you into the stinking back alleys of poverty, defeat . . . and death."

"You think you can scare me?" I asked in a voice that sounded, even to me, as though it was rattled by fear.

"Yes," she answered while managing to look very wise. "I think you have moved far from the old faith that you used to have in your Mama, but even so . . . even so. The Princess Astrial sees only truth and tells that truth just as she sees it."

"What is it you do see?" I asked, knowing full well that a person of genuine courage would rather have had their tongue cut out than even ask the question.

"That your success and happiness will come to you from belonging to something bigger than yourself alone.

Your first success will grow out of the family you were born into, and later on it will come from the family that you will marry into. Learn again to trust the princess and do whatever she tells you, and everything will be fine. And in your heart of hearts, you know that's true, don't you?"

I looked at her and wondered once again just why it is that God makes some people so sure of themselves while others never seem to be certain of much of anything. "I don't know what it is I know," I finally managed to answer. That might not be what anyone would call a wise answer, but at least I know it was a true one.

14

❧❧❧ I WENT BACK into the trailer only long enough to get my guitar, composition notebook, yellow pencil (the one with the eraser), pocket comb, and change purse before I was off again. Although I wasn't due at Mrs. McCaffrey's until nine thirty—about three and a half hours from now—I figured that anyplace would be better than this place.

On the far edge of the sky, the summer sun sat shyly while at the same time the branches of the elm and sycamore seemed strangely still. Gave me the heebie-jeebies. Sort of like everything—even nature—was waiting for God only knows what.

When I reached my spot on the river's edge, I thought that this would be as good a time as any to get some work done on my new song, "Bubba Baby . . . Baby Bubba." It's a country and western all right, but running through it is a wild and melancholy feeling that comes from the Gypsy in me. Most of my songs I've written here with my back resting up against this willow, but even after Lord knows how many tries, I still couldn't keep my mind on my work.

So I stood up, twirled my guitar from my front to my back, and began walking away. Among the river grasses there were colonies of assorted wild flowers, mostly thistles, silver bells, and dandelions. They looked real pretty growing there, and it doesn't take a graduate of agriculture from the state college to tell you that they serve a real purpose, too. For one thing, they help keep the topsoil from being washed away by wind and water.

When you get right down to it, nobody has much objection to things growing wild and things growing free as long as they know their place, keep to their place. Growing along riverbanks, edging the sides of dirt roads, or even fighting like hell for survival in the broken cracks of this town's concrete sidewalks. That's perfectly okay. So maybe the only unbreakable-unbendable rule is: Never set root, never dare to set root, where either cultivated crops or hothouse flowers bloom.

Wild flowers—weeds, call them that if you want to—

are a whole lot smarter than me and that's for sure. If they go crashing into somebody's garden, they know full well that it's only the farmer's duty to yank them unmercifully out.

But me? Me, I wasn't born with the sense that God gave a single one of them dandelions. Otherwise I'd never have come to believe that a wild flower like me could go anywhere my talent could take me. What a laugh! Maybe I should send thank-you letters to both Mama and Amber for setting me straight. First letter ought to go to Amber, 'cause she sure enough was born knowing that a Delaney weed doesn't belong in a Huntington garden. So just who am I to take offense when she, like Mama, yanked me up and out of where I had no right being? Just good common sense, if you ask me.

And so my dream of fame and glory was evaporating as swiftly and silently as an early morning dew, but for some reason that I couldn't put my finger on, I didn't feel all that bad. No, not so very bad after all.

Carlotta Dell. Carlotta Dell? The name sounded as though it came from a long-ago time and a faraway place. Names from old books with worn covers like Mother Goose . . . Hiawatha . . . Joan of Arc . . . Anne Frank . . . and Nancy Drew.

Struggling to reach the top, Carlotta might very well fail in full view of everyone who had ever been important to her. In front of all those who wanted to see her succeed and all those who didn't. So while attempting a spectacular triumph, she ran the risk of a painfully public defeat.

In a funny way, a way that I'd never really thought about before, Carol Ann had an easier time of it than

Carlotta, 'cause while her life wasn't exactly what anybody would call easy, nobody expects much of anything from Carol Ann. Leastways nothing good. And with parents like Gypsy and Painter to point to, it wouldn't even be thought to be my fault. How in this world could anybody be expected to succeed with parents like mine?

So that was it, wasn't it? Why I felt this sense of relief as though the pressure had just been turned off. Reckon when you get right down to it, it's better—safer, that's the word I'm looking for. Safer being Carol than Carlotta. So why shouldn't I go ahead and do what's expected of me? Using my music to help the Delaney Family Business while all the time pretending that that's exactly what I want to be doing?

I pulled up a ripe dandelion, pitting the full force of my breath against its holding power. All the featherlike pieces went blowing off in the wind except five, so I waited until I had a full supply of breath before blowing again. This time four yielded to my superior power and went flying. And so now only one feather, one stupid stubborn feather that knew more about fighting than it did about defeat, hung on.

Passing Loggerman's Liquor Mart, I heard my name being called. Through the screen door I saw the pink-faced Swede beckoning me in. Didn't he know he had the wrong Delaney? What on God's green earth could he want with me?

"Looks like you've gone and made the papers," said Mr. Loggerman, pointing to an inside page of the *Bainesville Weekly News*.

"Sir?" I asked, while checking out his face for even

the smallest sign of insincerity. If there were any clues there that he was pulling my leg, I couldn't find them.

"Right here," he said, striking one of the stories with his index finger. "They wrote you up just like you was the new Loretta Lynn."

PAINTER & GYPSY'S DAUGHTER SHOWS FINE TALENT

Carol Ann Delaney, the eldest child of Painter and Gypsy Delaney, is a high school senior who is preparing herself for a career in the dazzling world of show business.

According to her music teacher, Mrs. Chester ("Mac") McCaffrey, Carol Ann "is far and away the most gifted student that I've ever had the good fortune to teach. She's also the hardest working. Talent like hers does not come along every day or even every year."

Carol Ann, who sings and writes both the words and music to her mostly country and western songs, is busy as a beaver getting together a group of songs that she will soon audition before Mr. Jock Edwards. Mr. Edwards, owner of the Blue Note Recording Company in Nashville, Tennessee, is the man who started many of our favorite country and western singing stars off on the road to fame and fortune.

Mrs. McCaffrey was a sorority sister to Mr. Edwards' wife, the former Emily ("Lee") Pearson when she was at Arkansas State College. Mrs. McCaffrey says that there has been no specific appointment made for Carol Ann, but she has stated that there are "assurances that Carol Ann will be given every consideration at the Blue Note Recording Company when she is ready for her audition."

As our citizens in Bainesville well know, we are no strangers in this town to having our sons and daughters make names for themselves. This goes a long way in proving that this town is a lot more than just a wide place on the road.

In 1968 Lisa Caldwell, daughter of Mr. and Mrs. Sam Simon Caldwell, was second runner-up to Miss America. In 1972 Clive Russell, son of Mr. and Mrs. L. D. Russell, played shortstop for the Memphis Chickasaws. In 1981 Nannerl Overholser Keohane was appointed to the presidency of Wellesley College in Wellesley, Massachusetts.

All Bainesvillians will want to wish Carol Ann Delaney well as she begins her climb up the musical ladder of success.

I looked up into the transparent blue eyes of Mr. Cord Loggerman to see if I could find some proof there that the story was a good one. Oh, I know it sounds good, but I couldn't believe it. I couldn't believe it! Folks reading this could even forget some of the bad stuff and come to the conclusion that maybe I wasn't so bad after all. Especially I wondered if Amber Huntington and Will Bellows would read this and think that it was pretty good. I mean what the paper said about me.

I tried picturing Amber (it was hard) at least a teeny

bit sorry that she didn't allow us to become friends. And I tried picturing Will (it was easier) remembering that we had a real nice time together last November twenty-fifth at McDonald's, but that was six months ago.

One thing that I didn't have a bit of trouble picturing, though, was the source of that story. Mrs. McCaffrey had told me only a week ago about Lee Pearson, her best friend from her college days. "And as soon as Lee returns home to Nashville from visiting her daughter in Minneapolis, then I'm going to call her. Tell her all about you!"

Giving me two or three little pats to my shoulder, Mr. Loggerman nodded. "That's a good little write-up they gave you. Never in a million years would I have thought that ole Painter, of all people, would have a musical genius for a daughter. That's some surprise!"

"Well, I guess it's pretty nice what they wrote there," I said, feeling at the same time proud . . . and guilty. Why wasn't I defending my Papa from the Swede's judgment? Who does this seller of booze think he is anyway—some great humanitarian or something?

� 🌺 🌺

JUST BEFORE ENTERING Mrs. McCaffrey's screened-in side porch, I broke off a twig heavy with honeysuckles. I leaned back, making myself comfortable against the metal glider's fresh green cushions while biting off the tiny blossoms to suck up their sweetness. Trouble was there almost wasn't enough there to taste. Guess it was like a lot of things in this here life: the sweet being too little and too far between to be providing much of a taste.

Sooner than I expected, the side door opened. "Hope you're ready for your lesson." She wore a dress the color of ripe plums, and it made her look a little younger and softer than I remember her ever looking before.

She pointed to the folded section of the newspaper that was stuck beneath my arm. "Have you been reading all about yourself?"

I nodded. "Mr. Loggerman stopped me as I passed by. Gave me his paper."

"So? Well, what do you think?"

I could tell by the nervous smile that flitted across her face that she really was concerned about my reaction to the story. For a long moment, I didn't answer. Maybe I was allowing her to pay for a moment of sweetness in my life by an equal moment of anxiety in hers. It was a purely selfish thing, and yet I wouldn't have taken anything for it. I mean I can't remember the last time that anybody much gave a damn about what I was feeling.

"I thought it was real nice. Surprising as anything," I admitted. "But real nice."

"Oh, good," she said, sounding the relief not just in her words, but in her voice. "I honestly didn't realize it would make the paper when I went around bragging about you."

"You were bragging about me?" Considering the newspaper article it made sense, but still it was so hard to believe. Somebody actually bragging about me!

"Well, yes, of course. I told Marcia Michaels among others, and she told her daughter-in-law, Loretta, who is the reporter for the *News*. Then Loretta called to find out more, and I told her what she wanted to know, but I insisted that she call you for your okay before the story ran. Well, Tuesday night Loretta called back to say that she was up against deadline and that you didn't have a phone."

"Uh, those things you said about me . . ."

"Yes?" Her open face was encouraging, as though whatever question I wanted to ask she would very much like to answer.

"You really believe what you said? That I have talent? *Real* talent?"

"But you know I do! I've told you so, more than once."

"I know, I know, but I thought maybe you just liked to encourage your students . . . even your nonpaying student."

Jean McCaffrey laughed. "I only wish I had more students worth encouraging. Let me say this and maybe it'll help put things into perspective. Music has been a big part of my life, all my life. I'm sure I told you that my mother was a musician. She taught music at South Side High School in Memphis, and if she wasn't exaggerating, and knowing mother I don't believe that she was, she began teaching me music on the day I turned two."

"You were only two years old?"

"According to Mother. Well, over the years I've studied with a goodly number of people and I've taught a great many more, and I can tell you this: Every once in a great while a teacher will find someone with talent. Much more rarely, a teacher happens upon somebody with exceptional talent. And even rarer still . . ."

She reached over to let her hand rest on mine. "It happened to me only once—and that was teaching you, Carol Ann—I found a student with exceptional talent who was willing to go through all the time and trouble necessary to develop that talent."

I felt as though I couldn't possibly be hearing things quite right, and that any minute something would happen to show me up. Show me that it was all a joke. That I was all a joke. When is April Fool's Day? April, and it's already past. This is already May. Hot, sticky May twenty-first, remember?

"There's a word," she continued. "And Lord knows not a single one of my students can stand that word. But I think you can, because you have it, more even than your share. Talent without that dirty word 'discipline' is like a seed that was never planted."

I wanted to check out her face for sincerity, but I didn't have the courage necessary to raise my downcast eyes upward and expose my own face.

"Well, Carol Ann, you've got it both: the talent and the will to develop it, and I'm betting that that combination will take you far."

I think I felt Carlotta stir within me. Carlotta Dell, who, I could have sworn, up and died sometime after five o'clock this morning, just up and took a breath. So you're alive, are you? Alive, but not yet exactly alive and well 'cause you're still burdened by the Gypsy prophecy.

"You're very deep in thought, Carol Ann."

"Yes, I guess I am."

"Want to tell me about it?"

"Yes."

". . . Well?"

". . . It's kind of hard. I mean I don't know if you'll understand. I'm not exactly sure that even I understand . . . at least well enough to explain it to somebody else."

"We might be able to help each other understand."

I looked into her eyes and they reminded me of Gypsy eyes. Not in their color, not at all in their color, but in their ability to see below (or maybe it was just beyond) what eyes can normally see. I think I trusted Mrs. McCaffrey, but strictly speaking I know I wasn't supposed to. "We Roms never trust anyone who's not" is a phrase that I grew up hearing. "Well," I said, making that word fill in for an awful lot of silence, "it has to do with my parents, especially my mother. She's searched my palm—tarot cards and crystal ball, too—but she can't find any talent there. Says that nothing but bad will follow me if I follow my own career.

"What she wants—my father too—what they want is for me to go to work for them. It's sort of a—you could call it a kind of a family business. Well, according to Mama, it's only in this business that I'll find happiness."

". . . And you believe in your mother's ability to predict the future, do you?"

"That's not a simple yes or no question; sounds like one, but it isn't. Because the answer is actually sort of yes, sort of no. I mean sitting here with you, a nonbeliever, here in your living room, the answer is absolutely not! No, my mama can't any more predict the future than the man in the moon.

"But what about when I'm all alone, hundreds of miles from my home, and I don't know when I'm going to get my next audition . . . or my next meal. It'll be times like that that Mama's predictions will start weighing heavy on my mind."

I heard Jean McCaffrey sigh as though she had just come to some sort of unfamiliar junction on the road and there were no more road signs. Nothing at all to point the way. "I wish I knew what to tell you."

Remembering a story—a fairy story, I guess it was—from my childhood. All about a witch who places a curse on her very own child. And that child had to travel east and that child had to travel west before she found the mother of her spirit. The one whose love was strong enough to free her. "What you could tell me," I said at last, "is that my mother is all wrong. That my seeking after fame and fortune won't end in my dying. Promise me that nothing bad is going to happen!"

Then for the second time I heard her sigh, only this one, if anything, sounded even more despairing than the first one. "How can I do what you ask, Carol Ann? How can I replace your mother's downbeat prediction with an upbeat one of my own? Not when I don't for a moment believe that it's given to us mortals to know the future!"

What was I thinking of? What am I, some sort of baby who needs to press an outsider into being my mother? How could I have done what I did? Asking her for a guarantee of security in an insecure world? "I'm sorry. I didn't know what I was thinking about."

"Believe me, nobody can predict the future. Not me and not even your mother."

"You don't know anything about us Gypsies. Maybe it's possible that some of us might have powers."

"You're telling me that your mother has the power to predict the future?" she asked. Her tone was different, more aggressive now. She dug low into the pocket of her dress to bring out a thin wad of bills. "Fine. And here you are," she said, holding out two singles for me, "here's two bucks. The horses are running in Hot Springs; the Memphis Chicks are playing baseball in Mobile; and there's a play-off between the Boston Celtics and the Philadelphia 76ers for the division championship. Tell your mother to place this two-dollar bet for me. Let her demonstrate this great power of hers in a way that we can all see! And then everybody—even I will believe in her ability to predict the future."

"It isn't done like that," I explained, while shaking my head at the money that she held out.

"Take the money, Carol Ann."

"No."

"Come on, now, take the money."

"No, I won't do it!"

"Well, for goodness' sakes, why not?"

" 'Cause you'd lose your money, that's why. I don't believe that my mother could pick the winning teams if her life depended upon it, especially if her life depended upon it."

First she smiled and then she reached out and hugged me, and the thing was—the thing was, I didn't feel so alone anymore. "If you refuse, Carol Ann, to gamble somebody else's two dollars on your mother's ability to foretell the future, then why, dear Lord, are you willing to gamble your whole life away on the basis of that same ability? Or lack of ability?"

It was too big a thought to digest all at once. "I'm doing that?"

"Aren't you?"

"I don't know—maybe I am," I said, hearing a silent voice within echo, Yep, that's it. That's what I'm doing.

She gave my hand a squeeze. "Listen to me, Carol Ann. I don't feel comfortable making speeches, so chances are good I'll never repeat this, but for what it's worth, here it is: In my opinion, you have everything that it takes to make it in music. So with all your gifts plus a healthy run of luck, you might make it. You just might even make it big.

"Now the problem with luck is that it's so fickle. You can have it on Tuesday, but it leaves you on Wednesday. Additionally, it can't be bought, sold, bartered, bottled, or even predicted—especially not predicted! But you've got a chance at that jackpot, the one that sits right on top of the rainbow, and I pray to God that you take that chance. Give it everything you've got, and then spin the wheel."

For some reason I thought again about the young girl of the fairy tale who had to travel to the ends of the earth East and the ends of the earth West before she found her, the mother of her spirit. And when the child told her all about the curse that had been placed upon her, the beautiful lady reached into the sleeve of her gossamer gown, where she kept a wand capped by a flashing blue-white star. Waving that wand over the child's head three times, she spoke. "Let all the bells in the kingdom toll, for the curse has been broken. Send all the royal messengers out with the news: From this moment on, the evil spell has been broken and this child will live happily ever after. I so decree!"

❦ ❦ ❦ On Thursday, all seventy-three members of
the graduating class posed in the sweltering heat outside the
massive double front doors of Bainesville Regional High
School. As soon as that was done, Mrs. Constant made the
announcement for the second (probably the third) time to
"Make sure that you all carefully replace your cap and
gown inside the garment bag that is provided. And see that

the gown gets a good pressing before our graduation on Sunday afternoon."

With the plastic bag draped over my arm, I cater-cornered my way across the school grounds toward the highway. Funny thing was that I heard the attention-getting toot-toots, but I guess I never thought about them being for me.

"Going home, Carol Ann?"

Will Bellows, wearing a working man's tan and a T-shirt with a much-laundered replica of the Moosehead Beer label, opened the door of his lipstick-red GMC truck. "I've got to go pick up some supplies over at the feed store and then I'll drive you home."

"Oh, good, thanks," I said, leaning back against the blue plastic upholstery. "Did you hate all that picture taking as much as I did?" Actually I didn't either hate it or love it, but finding something to talk about with guys, or girls either for that matter, is not all that easy for me. Anyway, what I really wanted to know, I knew I wouldn't ask. But still it seemed strange that we had a good time to-gether at McDonald's, and yet we never did it again.

Will wiped the perspiration from his forehead with the sleeve of his shirt. "Jesus, I was sweating buckets under that gown! And that photographer, I wonder where they dug him up? I swear to God, he didn't know his ass from his elbow."

At the lights he turned right and drove all the way down Station Street to angle park in front of the red-and-white-checkered storefront advertising Ralston Purina Feeds. Moving his linemanlike body with all the quickness and agility of a quarterback, Will was out of the driver's seat and into the feed store. Wasn't more than a minute or two later, he returned carrying a burlap bag filled with at least a hundred pounds of something.

He started the engine while at the same time asking, "You really going to Nashville to meet a big time agent?"

"Guess you read about it in the paper?"

"Yeah, so you going?"

"Well, I'm not meeting a real agent like Colonel Tom Parker. I'm only going to meet the man who owns a big record company in Nashville. Mr. Jock Edwards."

"If Elvis was still alive, you think you'd have gotten to meet him?"

"Uhh no, but maybe some other singing stars, I don't know."

Will's pleasant, open face seemed suddenly to come scrunching together. "What do you want to be, a star?"

If I hadn't known better, I'd have thought that Will was mad with me for what I planned on doing, but that wouldn't make sense. Would it? "What I really want to do is sing and compose. Try my hand at popular and country and western music." But when his look didn't soften, I added, "Anything wrong with that?"

"Want to know what I think?"

"Sure."

"If you ask me, I think you're making a big mistake. You asked, so I told you!"

"But . . . but why?"

"Running around to Nashville, and God only knows where, and where's that going to get you?"

I thought about answering, "Tennessee," but it was plain that the last thing that Will wanted now was a little humor; so I just answered instead, "For one thing, I hope it'll make me a living."

"Think you need to do all that to make a living?" Will's face had taken on a kind of flush. Even beneath his tan you could still make out a very definite blush of color. "Is that what you think?"

"I don't rightly know what I'm going to need to do and what I'm not going to need to do, but I'm fixing to find out. Anyway, what are you getting so high and mighty about?"

"I'm not," he answered, while managing to hit every single bump on the dirt road that leads past the Frazer farm and comes to a stop about a mile farther on at our place. "Only if you go away, then we won't have time to get to know each other."

I knew that I was now going to ask him the question that for a long time now I'd been asking myself. "A whole lot of time has passed since our first date, Will. So how come you didn't use it to get better acquainted? I mean, if that's what you really wanted."

"Oh, I don't know—just been too busy I guess."

"Are you not so busy now?" I asked, hoping that his second answer would shed more light than the first one.

"Well, no . . . well, yes and no. It's just that I was thinking that now that I've got my diploma, I'm going to be running the farm. I'll get some help from my pa, but he's hurting with the rheumatism and I've got to be soon taking over the reins. And now that you've got your diploma," he continued, "it's time for you to settle down too, and pretending that you're going to be some kinda movie star ain't what you oughta be thinking about."

If I was any girl in Bainesville excepting Gypsy and Painter's girl, I might think he was edging close to a marriage proposal. But surely he wouldn't be proposing to me, now, would he? "Well, what exactly do you think I oughta be thinking about, Will?"

Will's words came rushing out so fast that some of them seemed joined. "That wecould doit together, you and me."

"You mean," I said, finally allowing the meaning to filter through, "the two of us?"

Will nodded as his granite-hard face took on a seriousness that I'd never before seen. "When I first heard you sing 'God Bless America' in the auditorium that day, I knew I liked you. I already told you that."

It was really "The Star-Spangled Banner," but small corrections didn't, at this moment, seem appropriate. "You did? Really?"

"Sure," he said, allowing a bit of tension to leave his face. " 'Cause, you know, you sing with a lot of sincerity in your voice. I like sincerity in a girl."

"I like it, too," I told him. "Especially in a guy. People with sincerity are okay in my book. Thing is, I don't hardly trust anybody without it."

"Me either!" said Will, looking into my eyes as though he was searching there for something that he had long ago lost. "So you want to get married or not?"

"Well . . . but we've only had one date."

"Doesn't take me long to know what I like. When I see what I want," he said, snapping his fingers, "then I make my mind up just like that!"

"I admire that too in a man," I said, thinking that my Papa isn't anything like that. Trying to picture him making decisions was real hard to do.

"You haven't seen the Bellows Dairy Farm," he was telling me. "But it's a good one. Fifty-two jerseys—forty-six of them are good milking ones—and we got us three hundred and fifty acres of some of the richest farmland in Dexter County. And the house, that's nice, too. The living room has knotty pine walls that my dad and I put up about six years ago. Never needs painting and it looks as nice now as it ever did.

"The bathroom has tile that comes up to your armpits and there's more than plenty hot water for taking showers or baths ever since we put in that new fifty-gallon O. A. Smith boiler last spring."

"Sure sounds nice as anything," I told him.

"The best thing," said Will with real assurance, "you haven't even heard yet. Our farm will never be subdivided after my mom and dad pass on. You see, I only have one brother, Jim, and he never took to farming. He's a chief petty officer in the Navy stationed up at New London, Connecticut, and my sister, Connie, lives in Dyersburg, Tennessee and she works for the telephone company and her husband . . . he sells insurance."

"Well, that's real nice, too," I told him, thinking that I must from this moment on strike that word from my vocabulary.

Will's forehead crinkled into rows. "What is?"

Was he beginning to suspect what I already knew? That I didn't know what to feel, think, or say, and especially not what to say. A marriage proposal was about the last thing that I expected to happen to me today. "Ohh," I said, playing for a moment of time. "Having an older sister. Somebody you can talk to when there's nobody you can talk to. I'm the oldest, so there's nobody for me to talk to."

"Connie's okay. I get along with Nick—that's her husband. He's ten years older."

"Than you?"

"Than her."

Then, within shouting distance of our trailer, Will steered his truck off the dirt road and onto the grasses, and then cut the motor. He turned to look at me and suddenly I thought: What lips! Exactly the way a man's oughta be: the right shape, size, and softness. He moved closer now, his face almost touching mine. And now I was breathing in the same warm, moist breath that he was breathing out. Kiss . . . kissed . . . kissing. Lost there among the kisses.

"Hmm," he said. "You kiss good."

"You too, Will. You really do!"

We kissed again, and then Will began laughing like he suddenly remembered something funny. "Once I took Amber Huntington to a track meet, but hey, I didn't like her all that much. That's one girl who thinks she's so fancy, living up there in the lap of luxury like she does, but have you ever tried kissing her!?"

Instantly we were both laughing. "What I meant," said Will, "was that I thought that kissing a fancy girl like that would be a lot like kissing blossom honey, at least as sweet as that, if you know what I mean."

"You mean to say it wasn't?"

"Nah, her mouth smelled like an ashtray full of butts on a rainy day."

"Ugh! I know what that's like, 'cause both my parents smoke and it stinks up the whole place, especially when it's damp or rainy. Wonder why it's so much worse on those days?"

Will pressed his lips together thoughtfully for some moments before replying, "There's a good scientific reason for it."

163

"Reckon so," I answered, while trying to figure out what single scientific principle could ever be broad enough to cover both the rainy-day stink of our trailer *and* the dank cigarette breath of Amber Huntington.

Funny. I must be a real funny person. Here I was getting my first (and maybe my last) marriage proposal that I'd ever in my life gotten, and by a real nice fellow like Will Bellows, and what did I do? Start wondering and worrying about some little scientific principle that nobody else would care beans about, that's what!

Thank goodness, though, Will didn't seem to pay much mind, 'cause he just went on talking about what good eyesight he had. "Good enough to track rabbit after sunset." How strong he was: "I know for a fact that there aren't more'n six fellows at Bainesville High who could win an arm wrestling contest against me. Probably Dave Sohier and Bobby McDonald and maybe a few of those super-beefy guys on the football team. But pound for pound, and I'm not bragging, I can wrestle anyone to the table."

Suddenly his eyes were staring almost pleadingly into mine. "I'm not just bragging, you know! You think I'm bragging?"

"No, I know you're not." I found myself smiling at him. Feeling a glow of warmth for him. After all, here was one big, strong guy who needed my reassuring words every bit as much as my little guy. My Bubba Jay!

And now there was not just one guy in my life, but two. One little . . . one big. Yep, he was okay, this Will Bellows. This Mr. William Bellows. World, may I proudly present Mr. and Mrs. William Bellows!

16

As I WALKED alone the final distance toward the trailer, I felt overwhelmed by okayness. Nothing to worry about 'cause everything's going to be okay. Okay! The only time that I remember feeling anything like this was that time when the nausea finally went away. It happened one evening last spring when I got sick, really sick, after eating that spoiled baloney.

I was so busy vomiting every few minutes that I could see that trying to sleep on the bed was might' near impossible. All I was doing was disturbing Bubba Jay and Alice Faye, so I stumbled out back to lie down among the tall grasses behind the trailer.

All through the night, I was so sick with the dry heaves, the wet heaves, and violent stomach cramps that I came right out and told God that he wasn't doing me any favors keeping me alive. What I think I had in mind was to make him so angry with me that he'd—POW!—strike me down dead, and then I would be eternally free of my misery.

Reckon, though, God didn't want me dead. He merely wanted me to want to be dead. Funny, I guess it was funny, but I don't think that I was afraid of dying nearly so much as I was afraid, desperately afraid, of dying alone.

Remember lying there on the damp ground throughout the moonlit night. My knees pressing up against my chest just like some not-yet-born babe. From time to time beneath my breath (and far too low for hearing), I'd call out, "When are you coming, Mama?" And once during a brief and fitful sleep I even dreamed she'd come to me with cool hands and concerned looks. Gently she had lifted my head while telling me to drink the ancient Gypsy remedy that she was carrying in a handleless cup. "Drink and all the pain will go. And, yes, all the sorrows, too."

"Yes, Mama. I'll drink. Whatever you say, Mama." Between sips of the bitter brew, I begged her to forgive me for all those things that I had done wrong. Especially for the wrong that I did in doubting her. "I know now, Mama, what I should've known then. You sure enough do have Gypsy powers. Powers aplenty to see the past, predict the future, and cure all sicknesses of the mind and body."

But when I woke, the stomach cramps were, if anything, more violent than ever. "When are you coming to me? Aren't you ever going to come to me, Mama?" But nobody came . . . and nothing changed. Nothing except the gradual shifting of the moon.

Hours later—I don't know how many, only that the night was retreating and the sun was fixing to take charge of the skies—it was then that just as suddenly as the sickness came, the sickness went. So as the day broke, I felt the first rays of the sun stroking me gently with its warmth. And with it came not just the absence of pain, but the presence of okayness. Everything was going to be okay! I had made it through the night.

🌷 🌷 🌷

PAPA, followed by Alice Faye, was walking quickly up the dirt road in my direction wearing a right unsettled look on his face. "Who was that in the red pickup that brung you home?"

"Will Bellows," I said, lifting up the plastic garment bag. "He was nice enough to give me a ride home, seeing as I had all this graduation paraphernalia to carry."

His ruddy face relaxed. "I'm sure glad you thought to keep him far enough away so he couldn't see that I was doing some sheet-metal repair on the coffin. Real smart of you."

"Thanks, Papa," I said, knowing full well that the real reason that Will and I stayed our distance had nothing to do with his need for privacy and everything to do with ours.

He pulled the protective eye goggles off their resting place at the top of his head. "I packed that cemetery soil down tight so it wouldn't show that the grave had been tampered with. Camouflaged it with real sod too, good enough so that a person wouldn't notice, but I can't get around the fact that it makes me nervous. The thought of it . . ."

The three of us walked over to where Mama sat cross-legged beneath the red maple while pulling a black satin ribbon in and out, in and out of a lacy pillowcase that was, without a doubt, meant for Baby Belinda. She looked up from the pillowcase only long enough to ask me the same question that Papa had asked.

But it was Pa who supplied the answer. "That Bellows boy—Will, that his name?" he mumbled before going back to work on the casket.

For the first time, Ma's face showed real interest. "Them's not the folks with the dairy farm?"

"Oh, yes ma'am, it sure enough is," I answered, while secretly hating what Mama seemed to be saying: that it was impossible (or maybe only barely possible) that somebody with money in his pockets could ever be interested in me. If only they knew. . . . "The Bellowses got themselves one fine house, fifty-two jersey cows, some of the finest farmland in all of Dexter county, and a fifty-gallon water heater that lets you take a hot bath anytime you get the notion."

"So what does that do for us?" asked Mama in a way that made it clear that her question wasn't so much a question as it was a challenge. "Fort Knox, so they say, is plumb filled to the brim with gold." She shrugged her shoulders. "But that don't mean nothing to us, neither."

Suddenly I felt lit—ignited would be closer to it—by

anger. Who's she to think that she was some beauty with a million boyfriends in her past? She's always bragging about them. Let's see now, there was: Ivan, the world's strongest man; Arturo, who played guitar for a traveling troupe of flamenco dancers; an eighty-seven-pound jockey from Paducah, and, of course, the one and only . . . Pat Patterson.

I stared right at her until our eyes caught. "Listen to me, Mama, and you'd better listen good! You always go around talking like you're some great, big, beautiful swan and me—me, I'm nothing but your poor ole ugly duckling. Well, Mama, you ought to know what everybody else does: You're not such a swan anymore, and me . . . it's plain that you haven't noticed, but I'm not such an ugly duckling, either."

In the nerve-shattering silence that followed, Mama stared straight ahead as though her eyes couldn't take in all that she saw. Or, maybe more to the point, it was her ears that couldn't take in all that she had heard. I was staring too, straight into those shocked, senseless eyes, and for the life of me I couldn't find her. Where was she? That magical mama of my childhood?

Way back then when she could perform six miracles in any seven-day week. And there inside her circle I could stay forever safe from all the witches and wizards and spells and curses in this world. And even in the world beyond.

So what happened, Mama? Who changed? And when did the miracles stop? Is it because a half-breed can never be more than just a half believer? Or was it that the magic was only there in the magic of believing?

So why, then, should I be mad with you? It's not fair

my being mad with you, 'cause you never really changed, Mama. Even with all your practice of the black arts, I was never safe and you were never there for me, not there when I needed you. Reckon the only difference is that I know that now. It hurts, but still I know that now. . . .

🌿 🌿 🌿

TURNING MY EYES from Mama, I looked out toward my river. Because of all the trees you can't see it, although you can, on a day like today, feel the soft river breezes. Without a word I sat down next to her and watched while she leaned forward to give her back a good scratching before returning to work on the pillowcase.

Half the time I was mad at her, and yet I couldn't one bit stand having her mad at me. I unzipped the garment bag to bring out the mortarboard. "Look, Mama," I said, placing it squarely on my head while trying to affect a bit of dignity. "Well, tell me what you think of your daughter now."

"Just great," she said, without actually bothering to turn her head to look.

So she was still mad, was she? Still licking *her* wounds? Well, let her! Reckon I've got wounds of my own needing licking. After a while she interrupted my thoughts about how to go about making up with her by asking an unexpected question of her own. "You really want to know what I think?"

As I tried to quickly figure out how much of a mistake it would be to come right on out and admit that yes—yes, I really did want to know what she thought—it was too late. She had already begun telling me.

"You think I spend too much of my time pretending to be a swan, do you? That's what you said? Well, unlike you, there never was a time that I didn't have men crying to marry me. There is a jockey from Paducah who has my name tattooed over his heart, and—"

I cut in. "Honestly, Mama, I don't know what this has to do with the price of potatoes!"

"It has a lot to do with it! 'Cause it's what I'd do if I were you: I'd forget about my music and I'd forget about wasting my time over at the McCaffrey woman's house. What does she have you doing over there? Scrubbing her toilets and cleaning her floors?"

"You're way off base, Mama! I haven't done a single thing for Mrs. McCaffrey, but she sure has done a lot for me. And something else: an hour hasn't passed since Will Bellows asked me to be his wife."

She looked hard at me to see if I was telling the truth or just some ole made-up lie. "Will Bellows asked *you* to marry him!?"

"You heard right, Mama."

Suddenly she grabbed hold of my forearm. "Some things you can kid about, Carol Ann, and some things you can't!"

"I'm not kidding; I'm telling the truth! Will Bellows asked me to marry him. Is that so impossible for you to believe?"

Releasing my arm, she began laughing. Laughing as though all the mean-spirited jokes that the world had for so long directed at her had, at this moment, come screeching to a halt. Through the marriage of her daughter, she would enter into the world of the respectable. But by the shrill sound of her laughter, I began to wonder just how she planned on treating all the others, all the outsiders. Any better than she had been treated?

Wrapping her arms around her body, she hugged herself tightly. "Mymymymy . . . now it's going to be our turn. Sticking our noses up higher than them that stuck their noses up at us." Then she made me promise not to mention a word of this to Pa, leastaways not till he finished the coffin. "Last thing we need is for him to stop working and to start celebrating with a chain of beers."

It was good to see her so happy, to know that I had given her happiness. I closed my eyes so that I too could wrap myself inside Mama's vision. I see myself walking inside Doc Finn's drugstore, just to look around and maybe even to spray myself with one of them sample bottles of free cologne. But this time he doesn't come rushing over to tell me that this here is a store for folks who want to buy things. "And so go on and do your looking outside!"

No sir, 'cause this time old Doc Finn is sweeter than a Hershey bar, 'cause as soon as he sees me he comes right over, slightly bowing his head as he speaks. "Howdy do, Mrs. Bellows. Something I can do for you today?"

"Ohh, no thanks," I tell the druggist. "I just came in to browse around. See what you got new."

"Well, you make yourself right at home." Then he points to the perfume counter. "And while you're here, spray yourself with our fine perfumes. Some of that stuff is mighty nice smelling."

And as I'm spraying and sniffing, first from one bottle and then from another, I hear my name being called. "Hi, there, Carol Ann—or aren't you talking to your old friends anymore? Now that you're Mrs. Will Bellows?"

Old friends? Amber Huntington an old friend? "Well, goodness gracious, how you doing, Amber?" I ask, suddenly becoming less than certain that the graying, hunched-over woman who now stands before me really is Amber.

"Ohh," she says with a wave of her hand. "I guess I'm okay. I've been living in New York, you know, but I don't think it agrees with me anymore. So I came back to Bainesville last week to see Mom and Dad. The folks, they're—well, they're so much older now."

"Last time I saw you, Amber, was on our graduation night, and you wore the most beautiful dress I'd ever seen."

"You mean to tell me—why, you don't mean to tell me that that many years have passed since we've laid eyes on each other?"

"Bainesville Regional High School graduation class of 1982 was when it was. You were voted the girl most likely to succeed and the most talented too, and there wasn't anybody who didn't know that you were one girl who was going to make it big. Boy, I just know that you must have impressed the devil out of those teachers at the design school where you went."

This time Amber shrugs while avoiding my gaze. After a moment, though, she replaces a sad look with a smile. "Oh, yes, if I had wanted to, I could have been a very famous designer with my name on the lips of movie stars and presidents' wives, people like that. But I was never interested in that stuff. I never wanted to be rich and famous, not for a minute! Anyway, tell me about you."

"You already know about me. I'm married to Will and we have two strong sons and two beautiful daughters."

"And I also know that everybody is always talking about all the blue ribbons your husband's livestock have won. Even my daddy, and you know how hard he is to please, says Will's got the best damn herd in the county. Hey, did you have any idea back then in those wonderful days at Bainesville High that so many fantastic things would happen to you? Way back then when we were such good friends?"

❦ ❦ ❦

S U D D E N L Y Mama gave my thigh a return-to-reality slap. "Know what I'm going to like a whole heap? All of us going over to your house and eating high off the hog just as regular as anything." She smacked her lips. "Imagine eating red meat when it isn't even a holiday! And then after my stomach is full to the gills, I might take it into my head to drink a cool glass of tap water. So I go on over to the kitchen sink and put a glass beneath the faucet without first having to move a lot of dirty dishes."

Pleasing Mama was pleasing me sure enough. Made me feel as though I had accomplished something, something worthwhile. "If I marry Will, do you think folks might start calling you Mrs. Delaney? Evangelina, or at least Evelyn?"

I watched her face quickly slide from pleasure to surprise and finally to anger. "What do you mean *if* you marry Will? You told me—you looked me straight in the face and told me that Will asked you within the hour to be his bride!"

"He did!"

I saw that beneath Mama's deep olive complexion enough blood was stirring to give an ever-so-slight reddish tone to her face. "You said *if* you marry Will. Now either he asked you or he didn't. It's got to be one way or the other. '*Yekka buliasa nashti beshe pe done grastende,*' which is a very old Romany saying that means, 'With one ass, you can't sit on two horses.'"

"He did ask me, Mama, honest, but—"

"Then why did you say *if? If* you marry him. I heard you say *if* just as plain as day!"

"The reason that I said *if* was because it was so sudden, coming like it did right out of the blue. So I told Will that I needed some time to think it through."

"Oh, you have to think it over, do you?" Mama's head bobbed up and down at the same time her neck pushed outward. "Well, you listen to me, Carol Ann, 'cause I'm not fixing to say this twice: If you ask me, all those things from all those books that you've had your nose stuck into have been mighty bad for you. Given you the wrong idea about how things are in real life. But I don't blame myself; the Lord knows it's not my fault! How many times, be honest now, have I said to you, 'Put down that damn book and come on over and watch TV with us'?"

"A lot," I admitted.

"And how many times did you?"

"Not a lot."

"Damn few, now ain't that the truth?"

". . . Guess it is."

"Well, if you'd been doing what I asked you to do, watching my afternoon shows with me—*Search for Tomorrow, As the World Turns,* and *General Hospital,* and things like that, then you'd already know a lot of things that you sure as hell don't."

"Mama, why don't you stop all this and just come on out and tell me what it is you want me to know?"

She sighed the way she sometimes does before tackling

175

a really big job. "What I want *you* to know? HA! What I want you to know is that real life is different than that stuff you read about in those thick books."

"How can you be so sure? You've never read a book, so how come you're such an expert on what's in them?"

"I didn't never go wasting my time with books, so that's how come I know enough to know this: Fancy daughters of fancy people can afford to sit back and think about offers of marriage. Them daughters of the high and the mighty. Sometimes even especially pretty daughters of poor men can think things over. But like I already done said, you ain't rich and you ain't pretty, so it sure ain't up to you to think things over. What we are talking about, Carol Ann, is them that glitter." Then she let her eyes slowly look me over. "And not them that don't."

"Mama, I'm going to tell you like I told Will. I'm going to give him his answer on graduation night, and I will."

"Never mind graduation night! You go hightailing it on over to Will's place right now . . . this minute! Tell him that you've had time aplenty to think about marrying him, and you've decided that you'd be pleased as anything to be his wife." Mama pointed a sharp finger in the general direction of the Bellows farm. "Go on now, before he ups and changes his mind."

I shook my head. "I'm telling you, Mama, what I've already told Will. I'm going to sleep on it and I'm going to give him his answer right after graduation on Sunday night."

17

❧ ❧ ❧ THE SATURDAY-MORNING sun burst across the eastern sky in such an unforgettable blaze of early-morning splendor that I know that nothing about this day will be forgettable. It's not that I'm saying that I'm certain that everything is going to be all hunky-dory. I stirred my morning coffee and looked out the trailer window into the newly breaking dawn to figure exactly what I did mean.

Mama has somehow managed to get not just Pa, but me, hopeful that the new Delaney Family Business will succeed. And before that sun falls from view in the west, we're going to have a pretty good idea whether or not Baby Belinda is going to make us money. But like Mama says, "This time it's going to happen, has got to happen, 'cause it's already time—past time for us Delaneys to be getting a lucky break."

It was my job fixing up all the food we'd be taking with us on this our first day of business. Placing thick cuts of Velveta on top of fresh slices of white bread and spreading yellow mustard on the second slice, I slipped all five sandwiches inside a used bread bag and tied it neatly with a wire twist.

Five eggs were bubbling and boiling inside a badly scarred enamel pot. A hard-boiled egg helps fill a person up when a sandwich alone can't do the job. There were only three smallish apples for the five of us, but Mama promised that the first money that Baby Belinda earned was going to go toward fresh fruit, luncheon meat, and Scooter Pies for everybody.

Outside I see Mama and Papa placing the folded old Army tent on the bed of the truck next to the coffin. Maybe it's wrong; maybe it's right; but it hasn't been bothering me all that much anymore. The coffin doesn't. Sure, she shouldn't've done it, but the good Lord knows that we five living Delaneys need that casket a whole lot more than the no-longer-living Sarah Jones. And since St. Sarah is the patron saint of the Gypsies, I wonder if our borrowing Sarah Jones' casket might not be a good omen, anyway.

I heard Pa calling my name. "Carol Ann, let's go! Bring the food and let's get a move on!"

Ma, Pa, and Bubba Jay sat in the warm comfort of the truck's cab while Alice Faye and I huddled together in the windy dampness in the back like chilled sparrows between two freshly painted signs, a tent, and of course Baby Belinda comfortably arranged inside Sarah Jones' newly restored coffin. As soon as Pa reached the highway, he began driving really fast, just as though he wanted to make certain that he'd reach Clarksdale before even a single one of them big Mississippi spenders left town.

From the cab, I could hear my Papa singing.

". . . When Irish eyes are laughing,
Sure it's like a melody . . ."

How long had it been since I'd heard him sing? How long had it been since he'd had anything to sing about?

I remembered back when I was very young, he used to sing to me all the time. Only to me, his firstborn. One song was about ears, that's right, ears! And it used to crack me up every time I'd hear him sing it. He used to start off singing very low, but gradually he'd get louder and louder.

"Do your ears hang low?
Do they wobble to and fro?
Can you tie them in a knot?
Can you tie them in a bow?
Can you throw them over your shoulder

Like a continental soldier?
Do your ears hang low?"

Truth is, I guess it didn't much matter to me what song Papa sang just as long as he did sing. With my eyes closed I could see him now as I saw him then. The sun gave highlights to his straw-red hair and I thought him the handsomest, most wonderful man in all the world.

One of my earliest memories is walking with him up toward where the river snakes. In one hand he held a fishing pole and in the other, he held my hand. "Too-ra-loo-ra-loo-ra," he began singing, "Too-ra-loo-ra-lay, too-ra-loo-ra-loo-ra, That's an Irish lullaby. . . ." I squeezed his hand tight because it was the only way I knew how to keep him with me . . . always.

Alice Faye huddled close to me and I put my arm around her to help ward off the damp winds. "I guess I oughtn'ta say I told you so, but I told you to take along your denim jacket."

"I ain't cold," she murmured, moving still closer. "Is the sheriff going to put us all into his jailhouse?"

I looked into my sister's thin face, her hair just a-blowing thisaway and thataway, but what I saw wasn't so much her hair but her fear. Seemed like a lot of fear to learn in only seven years. "Alice Faye, haven't I been telling you that you've been watching too many of those sheriff and bad people shows on television? Sheriff Long is only sheriff of one place, of Dexter County, Arkansas, and that's all! You know, once he leaves the county, he's not even a sheriff anymore. Only thing he is is plain ole Mr. Long and that's the God's truth. Now you know where we're going, don't you?"

"Clarksdale."

"That's right! And you know where that is? I mean what state it's in?"

The smile that spread across her face didn't leave space enough for anything like fear. "That's plumb over there across the state line, over there in Mississippi."

"Right again!" I told her. "And you know what Mama said she's going to buy you?"

"A Scooter Pie! We're all going to eat Scooter Pies in Mississippi!"

I hugged her to me. "We're going to have fun, eating Scooter Pies and not doing anything that would get a person into trouble with the law. Mama's not going to bless anybody's money. She promised me that! Only thing we're going to do is to give folks a sideshow, put a little excitement into their lives, and that's not even a little bit against the law."

"I don't think so, either," agreed Alice Faye, nodding her head with all the authority of somebody who is never—well, almost never—wrong.

Wasn't but a few minutes later that Pa turned off the road and began following the signs that read: THIS WAY TO THE FERRY. "This is going to be something, Alice Faye," I said, giving her hand a squeeze. "A cruise right across the mighty Mississippi River. You know this is the world's largest river?" Or was it the longest? The Mississippi is one and the Amazon is the other, but I forget exactly which is which.

Papa maneuvered his truck onto the ramp of the ferry directly behind a panel truck bearing a familiar logo along with the words *Tom's Toasted Peanuts*. Spill a small package of those peanuts directly into a cold Orange Crush, and you've got one of my mama's favorite meals. She even makes a joke out of it, calling it "my crazy Crush 'cause it's half nuts." Anyway, it tastes a little better than it sounds.

The ferry, which wasn't much more'n a motorized raft with a fence around the sides, held two trucks, three cars, and one black-and-chrome Harley-Davidson. But truth is, I wasn't half so excited by what was on the ferry as what was under it. The waters were more or less the color of strong coffee when a little milk is added in. Folks aren't one bit lying when they call it "the muddy Mississippi."

Just the same, I'd surely love to see her from top to bottom, from Minneapolis right down to the Gulf of Mexico. I'm standing here and soon I'm believing it, believing that there's nobody here but me. And I'm the captain piloting my very own boat with the yellow-and-white-striped awning with the fringe on top. Letting it float down to all those places that I've always dreamed of seeing. Know something, twin cities? You look just like you did in *National Geographic*. Sure, I would have known you anywhere, Minneapolis and St. Paul.

My boat's moving swiftly. Coming up on the right now is St. Louis in the state of Missouri. That's another one of Papa's songs. "Saint Louie woman with all your diamond rings . . ." Bye-bye, Missouri, and I'm back in my home state of Arkansas, but in a town I've never seen before: Osceola. Your football team has been beating our football team, but don't go getting smug about it. Sooner or later, you oughta know, all things change.

Hey! Hey! There's Memphis! You got yourself Beale Street, Graceland and The Cotton Carnival. And somebody I know was visiting your park and he told me that you've got yourself an ancient Egyptian tablet that came all the way from your namesake city of Memphis, Egypt.

Welcome to Mississippi . . . the hospitality state. Passing Greenville, and just up ahead is Vicksburg. Vicksburg was the scene of a famous Civil War battle . . . but it was the other side that won.

Louisiana. Louisiana Purchase. Phew, it's hot here, and sticky, too. If the gravity can't slow you down, then the humidity surely will, worse even than Arkansas. I can stand the heat of a hot day as good as the next person, but this would put a burn on the devil himself. I reach out beyond the sides of my canopied boat for handfuls of river water to throw against my body. That helps, doesn't it?

Bye-bye, Baton Rouge. Soon going to be nearing New Orleans! Bourbon Street . . . jazz and Al Hirt. One of my teachers—Mrs. Forrester it was—was once down there in New Orleans. Says that the land is so swampy that people have themselves buried above ground. If somebody besides Mrs. Forrester had told me that, I would have sworn that they were pulling my leg, but anybody who knows Mrs. Forrester will tell you that she's not exactly brimming over with a sense of humor.

South of New Orleans the breezes rush up from the Gulf of Mexico. The Gulf of Mexico! Just ahead is the last bit of earth before the Mississippi River merges with the still-mightier Gulf of Mexico, and from there it's a clean sweep into the vast Atlantic.

On the right, dotting the coast, are pastel shrimp boats, and perched back on the land is the white steeple of the Sacred Heart followed by three stores, each sharing a long corrugated tin awning. This Grand Pass, Louisiana, is a wee bit of a town, not so much a town as a hamlet. Still, what choice do I have? I must cling to the mainland. So this has to be it, where my scenic river journey must end. This is where I must give up my float-along existence and come face to face with life. The way they say we're supposed to live it.

Why am I crying? And why did I go on pretending that a downriver adventure could last forever? Rivers are like anything else, everything else, they all come to an end. Come to an end too soon. All right! All right, enough of these tears! And there it is: the last boat slip on the very last sliver of land on the North American continent. Head your boat there. Come on now, do what I tell you!

It's not really all that much to be sad about. I don't know why you're carrying on the way that you are. Crybaby, don't you know that everybody's got to cling to the land? Land is where they've got all those road signs, generation after generation of road signs. Telling you where you can't go and where you can and at exactly what rate of speed.

Okay, so you've had your fun and now do the only sensible thing: turn the tiller to the right, and I'll be off the waterways and onto the roadways. Move it quickly. Quickly! And before long I'll be speeding up and down the superhighways of life just like everybody else.

Yet unlike anybody else, I only stared at that tiller without actually touching it. Stared at it until my eyes blurred while all the time telling myself that all I had to do to stay safe was to reach out and turn that tiller. Turn it. Come on, turn it now! Now before I'm out beyond the safety of the river and into the mighty waters of the Gulf.

Beyond the point where small crafts ought to wander. Now! Now!

But the only thing I did do was nothing. Nothing except lean far back into the little boat, fold my hands across my chest and close my eyes. And I didn't open them again until I felt the swell of a really great wave crashing against the hull. The kind of wave that no river nowhere could ever create.

18

❧ ❧ ❧ By nine o'clock in the morning on a grassy spot on the side of the road somewhere between Clarksdale and the Helena bridge, the Delaney Family Business was born. Approximately a hundred yards down the highway from our tent, two large signs were hammered into the moist earth.

Stimulate Your Senses!!!
Educate Your Mind!!!
* * *
SEE
The AMAZING
The INCREDIBLE
B * A * B * Y   B * E * L * I * N * D * A
The dead child with
Growing Hair
& Growing Nails

(Just Ahead in the Army Tent)

The second sign read:

FUN!   FUN!!   FUN!!!
For the Entire Family
Be Educated . . .
Be Amazed . . .
* * *
S * E * E the Dead Child
With the A * L * I * V * E Hair!!!

(Just Ahead in the Army Tent)

The only really hard thing that we had to do was to
lift the very heavy casket from the truck and then onto
the wheels that would take Baby Belinda into the tent.
But Mama even made that job easy by asking some passers-

by for help in exchange for what she described as "A real sincere look at our beloved Baby Belinda. Truly one of the great wonders of the modern world."

After the still-closed coffin was placed exactly where Mama directed, she looked straight at the two men. "You will wait outside the tent until you are called. The child must be prepared for guests."

The younger of the two men, who was just beginning to show the signs of a beer belly, looked very uneasy, as though he didn't know what to think, least of all how to behave. At first he acted embarrassed, like he was the butt of a crazy Gypsy joke, and at the next moment he seemed as solemn as if there had been an unexpected death in the family.

Then suddenly, grabbing hold of his belly, he jumped the narrow gully separating this piece of land from the highway and took off running. The older man went flying after him, yelling, "Mel! Mel! You all right, Mel?"

Mama stuck her head out of the shadowy tent looking every bit as puzzled as I've ever seen her look. "Where'd they go? Why did they go running off without seeing the baby?"

I looked at her while thinking that sometimes—like now—she reminded me of a baby. Not because she looked so young. No, that wasn't it at all. It was because she looked so . . . so vulnerable. Like maybe she, too, needed comforting. "Well, there's no need getting upset, Mama," I told her. "It doesn't mean anything. Besides, they weren't exactly paying customers, you know."

"The girl's right," agreed Papa. " 'Cause some men have weak stomachs don't mean that we won't get our share of the business."

As the tears welled up in my mother's eyes, her hands clenched up. "Give away something for free and nobody notices it! They never do, the dumb rednecks! What do *those* people know? Give them the chance to see a true miracle of nature and what do they do? But do I care? I don't care because other people—a lot of other people—are going to pay out good money to see our beloved Belinda. I haven't lost not one ounce of confidence," she said, snapping her fingers. "You'll see!"

Just then, on the opposite side of the highway, a panel truck belonging to the telephone company rolled off the highway and onto the grassy shoulder before coming to a complete stop. The driver poked his suntanned face outside the window for some moments before climbing out to walk directly toward us. He smiled, a little cautiously, I thought, before asking, "What do you all do? Give showings?"

Mama returned his smile, but with a sense of majesty that would tell anybody that she not only knew who she was, but where she came from. Roots. From the other side of the centuries. From one thousand years of Gypsy history. "We do, sir, but only to people who shine with an inner spirit of enlightenment. Do you, sir, thirst after knowledge?"

"Oh, yes ma'am," he said, visibly snapping to attention. "Every bit as much as the next man."

"Fine, oh very fine. The exhibit is entirely free, but we do request a two-dollar donation. This money is not for us, but goes directly to England to help support the grieving parents of Baby Belinda."

For a long moment the phone man turned to stare back at his truck before suddenly pulling out his wallet and counting out two single dollar bills. "Something wrong with the parents?"

With her index finger, Mama tapped the side of her head. "Poor Lady Pamela has never been the same since she lost her beloved Belinda." Without so much as a break in the conversation, Mama shot me our prearranged signal to begin playing and help get the man's mood changing. "Lord Harold always has to keep someone with her. Nurses around the clock, and that doesn't come cheap."

So, strumming my guitar sadly, I preceded him into the darkly lit tent, where he whipped off his blue baseball cap as a sign of respect before coming to an awkward stop directly in front of a rope barrier less than six feet from Baby Belinda's bier. A single altar candle flickered softly at her head, throwing highlights on her long and luxuriant golden tresses. I began to sing:

> *"Swing low, sweet chariot,*
> *Coming for to carry me home. . . .*
> *I looked over Jordan*
> *And what did I see,*
> *Coming for to carry me home? . . ."*

After the song ended, the still hatless man walked back through the tent's opening, all the time shaking his head in wonderment. "Now, don't that beat all! Her hair's really long now. How long was it when she died?"

"Bald like most any baby," explained Mama. "Lady Pamela hated it. Said it made her daughter look like a boy, but Lord Harold liked it thataway. You see, he never had what he wanted most—a son. So Lady Pamela sort of humored her husband along 'cause she knew it wouldn't be long before her child grew herself a beautiful head of hair. And then not even Lord Harold could pretend that their beloved Belinda was anything but a girl."

The phone man hadn't got back into his truck before Mama had pulled out the bills from beneath her blouse and danced around and around with them. "This is only the beautiful beginning," she said, stopping just long enough to place a passionate kiss right smack-dab in the middle of George Washington's unsmiling paper face. "We're onto something big. Big! I tell you!" Then she began to dance again. "Didn't I tell you that?!"

"Mama," I said reaching out for the money, "can I drive the kids over to the supermarket for a bag of oranges and maybe even one of those Scooter Pies they've been dreaming about? I think we have enough money for that."

"Ohh, no you don't," she said, looking at me as though I had taken leave of my senses. "Your Papa can take the kids over to the market, but you, you I need here."

I wanted to be with them, especially Bubba Jay, when they finally got something that they really wanted. I had to see their faces, join in on the excitement. "You don't have to worry, Mama, I'll be right back."

She looked directly up as though she was fixing to speak to some low-floating clouds. "Help me get it through this girl's thick head, Lord, that I need her here. Need her to play her music and set the mood for the suckers. And let it stick there in that head that nobody spends money unless they're in the right mood."

"Okay, Mama, okay!" I said, feeling at the same time proud to be needed and ashamed that I needed to do what

I did. I mean I pretend to myself that it's only show biz and so don't mind fooling people, but still . . . I mind fooling people.

Then, from the side of the road, we heard a little loose gravel crunch and we all looked up to see a car so old that it had a running board. "What you got in there?" called out an elderly man from the car's window.

Mama moved toward him wearing a smile so serene that it would have put a reigning queen to shame. "What we have here, sir, is such a great mystery that it ranks as one of the great wonders of the modern world."

"That so?"

From so few words, I couldn't tell if he was being sarcastic or merely interested. My mother must have taken the optimistic view, 'cause she went right on with the sell. "Inside our tent is a child who was killed by a bomb during her own christening." Ma looked heavenward as though she was, at this very moment, trying to make eye contact with God. "The firstborn of Lady Pamela and Lord Harold Ashburton. Forty years after that there Nazi bomb fell on that English church, the child's hair and nails have kept on growing . . . and growing . . . and growing."

The man got out of the car leaving a very old lady still sitting inside. "Got to see this for myself," he said, striding purposefully toward the tent's entrance. But even more suddenly, Mama appeared in time to block the way. "If it was up to me, I'd let you see Baby Belinda for free, but I only take orders from England, and so I'm going to have to ask you for a two-dollar donation. It's to help out Lady Pamela in her time of great need."

"Two dollars? It oughtn'ta cost that much to see something already dead."

Mama nodded understandingly at the same moment she gave me the signal to begin playing. "Tell you what. I have a soft heart, so we'll just say three dollars and you can take your wife in, too. Just don't mention it to anyone in England. Three dollars for the two of you. How's that for a good deal?"

But the old man shook his head vigorously. "What do I want to take her for? That old lady hasn't had her wits about her since the summer of seventy-six."

Mama threw her hands up in a gesture of surrender. "Okay, okay, I'm not used to dealing with such a good bargainer. Look, I'll tell you what: I said three dollars for the two of you, but we'll split that right down the middle. A buck fifty for you alone."

"Fifty cents," countered the old man. "And not a penny more! The picture show and the bowling alley, they all give me my senior citizen discounts."

For some reason that totally escaped my reason, Mama looked dumbfounded by the old man's words. "Are you kidding me, sir? Don't go telling me that you've already reached your sixty-fifth birthday!"

"Yep," he said, letting his chest swell. "Reached it nearly twenty years ago, 'cause come next September, I'm going to be eighty-five years old."

"Well, I'll be doggoned. You look so young! Charles!" She waved Papa over. "Charles, come on over here and look at a man who looks a good thirty or thirty-five years younger than he really is."

As Pa agreed wholeheartedly with every word Mama uttered, the old man suddenly looked as though he hadn't felt this good in at least that many years.

Mama dropped her arm around his frail shoulder while

she spoke to him in friendly tones. "Hey, tell you what I'm going to do. I'm going to let you see our beloved Baby Belinda for a mere fifty cents. Plus . . . plus for that very same fifty cents, I'm going to give you and your money both a very special blessing. Helps to make the folding stuff grow and multiply."

Striking a loud, harsh note on the guitar, I threw dirty stares at Mama and then stopped playing. But all the while the old man beamed. "You mean to tell me you're not going to charge me a penny more for all of that than you were for showing me the baby alone?"

"That's right," she told him. "That's *so* right." And the smile that Mama returned to him must have been the same one that Delilah used when she told Samson to trust her to take care of things while he got himself a little shut-eye. Then, with Mama's arm still wrapped protectively around his aged shoulder, they both disappeared inside the tent's opening.

❦ ❦ ❦

AT SIX-THIRTY in the evening, almost thirteen hours to the minute after we left home, we loaded Baby Belinda, one tent, two signs, and all five of us Delaneys into the truck to head for home. But not exactly straight home. The first stop was Tommy's Discount Liquors, where Papa excitedly explained the savings over Loggerman's, tapping the side of his head. "I'm playing it smart. I'm getting me a case of beer."

The second stop was the Edwards' supermarket, where *I* was also determined to play it smart and stock up. Pulling out a tightly wedged cart, I told my folks, "I'm spending the rest of our money—all seventy-five dollars on groceries, okay?"

Throwing up her hands in a the-sky's-the-limit gesture, Mama said, "Stock up. Stock up! Buy what you want, just don't tell me nothing about that thin-lipped home ec teacher of yours. Bet that gorgio never made eighty-seven dollars in a single day. I can bet you that."

"No, reckon she never did." And yet didn't Mrs. Constant make a living every working day of her life? Just the same, I guess I was pretty awed by being on what you might call personal terms with so much money.

While I tried to get the best possible value for every dollar spent, Mama, for the most part, just walked alongside of me talking on and on about her bigger and bigger plans for the Delaney Family Business. "For one thing, we're going to get some more signs made up. Stick them up as far as a mile on either side of the tent. Most people zoomed up and down that road so fast, they didn't even see us."

"Still, we did all right," I answered, although I was really more interested in trying to figure out which was the better buy: the ham in the tin from Denmark or the cellophane-wrapped ham in the store's freezer.

"Another thing we're going to need are lights so we can stay open longer hours." Mama swept her hand above her head. "Battery-operated lights that blaze across the nighttime sky telling everyone for miles around that our Baby Belinda and our captured Martian Marvel are out there waiting for them!"

I picked up a large bunch of mustard greens and placed it in my cart before experiencing a reaction. "Captured Martian what?!"

She grabbed my hand and squeezed it until it hurt. "You don't think your mother is just going to let things drift along, do you? Not now that she's found the true secret of success!"

"No, I guess not."

"Oh, boy, are things ever going to be different for us!" Then, right in front of the frozen pizza, she turned to face me. "Finally everything's just a-looking up for us, Carol Ann. The business and Will Bellows—and do I have to tell you, of all people, how important this is?"

I answered, "No ma'am," while trying to avoid her all-seeing Gypsy gaze. But if everything was as great as she said it was, then why didn't I feel all that great about everything? I told myself over and over that what we were doing wasn't all that terrible. Well, it wouldn't have been if Mama had drawn the line at stealing. Outside of the blessing of money, we weren't doing anything bad. For a medium amount of money, we were giving folks a little excitement along with a lot of suppertime conversation. At least that's what I wanted to believe.

That made me sick, what Mama did to that old man today, but after I put my foot down, she promised never again. I told her that I absolutely, definitely wouldn't play the guitar if she ever mentioned the term "blessing of money" again. And she promised me on a stack of Bibles that she wouldn't. Not again, she told me. "Never never again!"

Mama had gone right on talking. Reckon I was too busy

with my own thoughts to take it all in, but just the same I got the drift. All about how finally, after all this time, this family had got its chance. A chance like we never had before and how me and my guitar playing were a real important part of the chance.

"So just because you and Will Bellows is going to be hitching up," she was saying, "that don't mean—that don't for a minute mean you can give up the business. Oh no, you can't no more give up the family business than you can give up your blood. Your Gypsy-Irish blood!"

19

❦ ❦ ❦ I T W A S a toss-and-turn night. Or it would have been if there had been enough bed space between Alice Faye and Bubba Jay for a little more tossing and a lot more turning. Without moving, I tried seeing through the darkness, trying to see those familiar things that I couldn't possibly see.

For all these years I had seen these household objects

day in and day out. Mostly seen them without actually looking at them. Still, after all this time, they should be etched so deeply upon my brain that I could picture them down to the smallest detail without even a bit of morning light.

Damn it, who cares!? What is this with me anyway? I mean every time I have something serious that demands to be carefully thought out, I just up and play mental hooky instead.

Here I am in the already wee morning hours of my graduation day and I'm not one bit closer to a decision now than I was at that very moment when Will Bellows first asked me to be his wife.

Let's see now, the ceiling fixture has this thin molding around it. Wood molding, or it may really only be plastic and made to look like wood. Probably it's blond molding, but it could be darker than that. Enough, stop junking up my mind! Do something useful, go back to that song that's been skitting and flitting about my brain. Sometimes when I'm working on a song the music comes first, and sometimes it's the lyrics. But this little ditty is unusual 'cause the words and music are coming together.

> *Willy . . . oh, Will-he,*
> *You're driving me daffydilly.*
> *Willy . . . Oh, Will-he be mine . . . ?*

Stop it! Stop this. . . . I should be thinking, not writing music; but trying to decide what to do when I don't have the foggiest idea what I ought to do is driving me daffydilly crazy and that's the truth.

What I ought to do is to take advantage of all the good

luck that's trying mighty hard to come pushing my way. Why, anybody born with the sense that God gave a toad would know exactly what to do. It's as plain as the nose on my face. If I marry up with Will, then I won't have to struggle and strain and most probably fail on my way to becoming special. Cause marrying Will will automatically make me special. Presto!

'Course, Mrs. Will Bellows doesn't have quite the glitter to it that Miss Carlotta Dell does. Still, it sounds a lot better than you-know-what. Being me. Being Miss Carol Ann (less than nobody) Delaney.

Ever so slightly, I wiggled up to a sitting position before going forward on all fours to crawl down to the foot of the bed. The screen door squeaked as I gently pushed it open and went out into the not-yet-born morning. From the Frazers' west field there was the smell of land freshly plowed. Soon as the ground dried a bit, they'd be planting it with wheat, which looks good growing and smells good, too. Still, nothing smells as mysterious and, at the same time, comforting as the dark, rich earth.

I looked skyward into the same man-in-the-moon face that I used to spend hours talking things over with years ago when I was little. "Hey there, ole man, remember me? The skinny girl who was always carrying a book or two and lived in a trailer, just south of the Bainesville town line?" I laughed to myself, or maybe it was at myself. A person would have to be pretty loony—pretty desperate is more like it—to carry on a conversation with the moon.

Going after musical stardom is what folks around these parts would call "pie in the sky," while marrying Will is like "pie on the table." There—that ought to make the choosing easier. Maybe if I married Will, then I'd have myself a real honest-to-goodness living, breathing human talking-with-me person. Then I'd stop carrying on these dumb conversations with the moon. Sure I would, because if I were married to Will, then I'd never have to be lonely again.

By the time I reached my spot on the river's edge, I had decided to figure by mathematics what I couldn't, for the life of me, seem to figure by my head or heart. Anything, try anything that might get me out of this mental kettle of glue. The fingers on my right hand would count all the reasons why I should marry Will, while the fingers on my left hand would mark off the reasons why I shouldn't.

Let each finger represent one voter, then the election goes to the side with the largest number of voters. What could be more democratic? It's the American way.

I stuck up my right thumb. "Marrying Will Bellows is the absolute sensible thing to do."

Next my right index finger. "It's what Mama wants. Like she said, she can't run the Delaney Family Business without my help. Oh, Papa, she explained, can help with the heavy stuff, all the loading and unloading. But she needs me for the music and all the other creative stuff."

Then tallboy, the middle finger. "The kids, sure as shooting, need me to help look after them. Don't know why Mama never took much interest in what they put in their mouths or on their backs."

Fourth finger: "Will wants it."

Pinky: "Marrying Will will give me a place in this world that's all my place."

Then with all five fingers on my right hand outspread,

I raised my left hand before the freshly dawning morning sun. And for moments—it seemed longer than mere moments—my thoughts were so scrambled up that I didn't have any way to express it, not even to the moon. "Well, the hell with this and the hell with voting, too!" I jammed both hands into the pockets of my cut-off jeans and began walking back toward home. "Truth is there's not a single, solitary reason why I shouldn't be jumping at the chance to marry Will Bellows."

Then beneath my foot a branch dried out by time and the weather cracked so loudly that I had trouble for a moment remembering my thoughts.

"Oh, yes, I remember now. There's five votes for the marriage and not a single vote against it. At least not a single no voter who has had the courage to speak out. And so that's that. The majority rules!

"Wait a minute. Wait one damn minute! All the yes voters were given time a plenty to speak out, so why not me? Me, the lone no voter?"

I waited, but only silence followed because there were no words. At least no words or strings of words that I knew that could come anywhere close to saying what somehow I felt needed to be said.

But the smart part of me—reckon it was my majority rules part—began drowning out the silence with angry shouts. "All your fancy talk about wanting to say your piece and what do you do? Stand there speechless with that dumb hound dog look on your face. Well, I've been around long enough to know your type. All talk and no action.

"Okay, you can think all you want to that I'm not talking 'cause I've got nothing to say, but you'd be wrong. Oh, you may be right enough in thinking that I don't talk out loud so good. But that don't mean that I don't feel what's inside me true enough. 'Cause I do. I feel it powerful strong.

"It's about what I need." I heard myself sigh as though the heaviness of my words had plumb near worn me out. But just the same, I struggled on. "It's about who I am—what I am. When you've been common all the days of your life, it's not enough anymore, not good enough to just marry into specialness. Not even good enough to go back—even if I could—like Amber Huntington and be born into specialness.

" 'Cause when you've been without it all the days of your life, then it looks like nothing will ever take the place of becoming special on my own. Come hell or high water, nothing is ever going to feel right until I make it on my own. Until somehow, some way, I learn to make my own specialness."

As I looked up at hands thrust up against the splendor of the rising sun, I knew that my words were true. And yet that single raised finger of the left hand was both out-numbered and out-gunned when compared to all five out-stretched fingers on the right.

20

❧ ❧ ❧ As I followed a black-robed graduate while another black-robed graduate followed me, I thought the Bainesville Regional High School auditorium had never before looked so . . . so dignified. Probably more than the huge center-stage bouquet of gold and white chrysanthemums, it was the majesty of Sir Edward Elgar's "Pomp and Circumstance." Chalk one up for another one of us composers.

Walking up the center aisle, I began searching the sea of faces for my folks. I'm sure they're here by now, probably with even more money thanks to the new Delaney Family Business. When I left our roadside business there was already forty dollars dangling from a cheesecloth bag between Mama's breasts, plus a piece of paper from me with the time and place of this ceremony. It was signed "With love from Carol Ann," and there was a P.S., too, that said, "See you then!"

I was about thirty miles from Bainesville when I hitched a ride back this morning at eleven A.M. from a Wonder bread driver. Though why Mrs. Constant insisted that we graduates had to be here a full two hours before the start of the ceremonies is something that I'll never understand.

Anyway, the Wonder bread man spent almost the entire ride telling me that it was positively against company policy picking up hitchhikers. I tried to make him feel more comfortable by reminding him that he agreed to give me a ride after stopping to see Baby Belinda, and so the company ought not feel all that bad about it.

That seemed to cheer him up so much that he ripped open a large cardboard box to present me with the Wonder bread company's best product: a free package of golden Hostess Twinkies. I, for one, didn't have to ask him about the company's policy about that.

Now I was approaching the stage as Elgar's music thundered triumphantly on. Once I took my seat on one of those metal folding chairs, then I'd be able to find my family. What I wanted to see was their pride in my accomplishment. Didn't matter how far back they might be sitting in this auditorium, I had good enough eyesight to find them.

Besides, I knew what to look for 'cause pride sometimes shows in a special set of the mouth and a special crinkle to the eyes. And although it was Mama who went out of her way to pretend that education didn't mean much of anything, I was the first Delaney or Yergis to ever have graduated from high school. Anyway, I guess I just knew that when Mama saw me accept my diploma, she'd be wearing that certain smile.

Suddenly there was a poke to my rib and I thought: What am I doing wrong? Maybe sitting in the wrong chair? But when I turned toward the poke, I saw a piece of lined paper folded to about the size of a book of matches being held out to me.

At the same time that Freddy Barton handed me the note, he gestured that I should look just behind me to the left. And that's when I saw him. Will Bellows busily raising and lowering his eyebrows as though they were being controlled by some crazy but invisible puppeteer. In spite of myself, I laughed as I unfolded the penciled note and read:

Hi Love:
    I can't wait to celebrate!
    *Meet me at the truck as soon as this is over. I want to drink Schlitz and talk about US!!!
                        x x x
                        Will

* Be right back for C.A.D. soon as
I drive my folks home!

As I smiled over Will's show of affection, there was another poke to my rib, only this time it was a red mechanical pencil. I took it and wrote:

> Will—
> Me too!
> Carol Ann

Funny thing, he doesn't seem to be in one bit of suspense about what my answer is going to be. Best as I can gather, he believes that hungry folks won't turn down a roast beef dinner and a poor Gypsy girl won't turn down Will Bellows. Just the same, I can't help admiring that in him. He's much more sure of what my answer is going to be than I am.

Probably he's right, but I won't know for sure, not until tonight. Although I've given up trying to force an answer on myself, I've stopped worrying about it, because there's no way that I can get through tonight without a decision, that's for sure!

After passing the note back via Freddy, I went back to listening to Mr. Hoyle, our school superintendant. ". . . and that's why, ladies and gentlemen, I first wrote a letter back during the first week of school asking this famous television evangelist to deliver our commencement address. To tell you the truth, I didn't hold out much hope that he'd actually accept. So it's with a great deal of pride and humility that I now turn the speaking chores over to our illustrious guest, the one and only . . . Reverend Jimmy George Johnson!"

Suddenly the whole auditorium was exploding with applause as the tall man with hair the color of silver strode purposefully toward center stage to take command of the podium. I was clapping pretty hard myself because, for one thing, this was the first time that I had been anywhere near anybody famous. Oh, once when he was running for reelection, I heard Senator Bumpers speak at Bryant Park, but I was kind of far back in the audience and not up close like I was now.

As he walked by me, he was close enough that I could catch a brief whiff of his cologne, all spicy and nice. But I'm sure that even those outside of smelling distance were impressed as anything with him. Besides his height and his hair, there were his clothes. A dazzling white-linen suit with a vest, a royal-blue shirt, and a white-and-blue-striped tie. In Bainesville, at least, the only middle-aged man who ever dressed to dazzle was Roland Price. And nobody, as far as I know, has seen the likes of Roland for a long, long time. Ever since he was run out of town. Folks said he was a pimp.

Before the Reverend Johnson got started talking about the subject of his speech, "Christianity: A Healing Salve to a Troubled World," he began thanking everybody in sight and even one person who was nowhere in sight: his mother. ". . . don't know what I would have become if I hadn't had Mom, keeping me on the paths of righteousness."

He went on to describe a blow-by-blow battle that once went on between his mother and the devil for his immortal soul. "Yes, ladies and gentlemen . . . believers in Jesus Christ, it was my blessed mother who fought for my soul, and that's what I'm trying in my television ministry to do for you . . . and you . . . and you."

And then for a long and expectant moment, he fell silent, as though allowing time for his healing words to be soaked up by his spiritually parched listeners. Much in the same way that it takes dry, cracked soil time to absorb the wondrous blessing of rainwater.

Then suddenly his arms did a skyward sweep, and right off I took it to mean that the sights of the Reverend Jimmy George Johnson were moving from the purely personal to the strictly global.

Between my search for my family and my unsettled thoughts about Will, I listened to the preacher long enough to know that he was "vehemently opposed" to the teaching of the theory of evolution in "our Christian schools. Let them know now and let them know forevermore . . . that we will never allow Darwin along with Jews and other atheists to rewrite our Bible."

At that point I didn't applaud, but some people both in the audience and on the stage did. What I did do, though, was to turn ever so slightly to look at a half dozen or so seats over to the left at the only Jew in our graduating class, Mark Feinberg. His parents, Rose and Jerome Feinberg, have owned the nicest store in Bainesville for a lot of years. As far back as I can remember, anyway. Without lifting his hands or lowering his eyes, Mark seemed to fixate a frozen stare on the evangelist with the wildly-waving arms.

Although I've never had what you might call a real conversation with Mark, I did want to talk with him now. I wanted to tell him that I really hoped he didn't feel bad, because lots of times majorities go around acting thataway. Like they've got to be very fearful of us few, of us minorities.

The last person on earth that I would have ever expected to learn that from was the very person I did. Although I guess it's fair to say that the lesson was lost on the teacher, but not on the student. No sir, not on this student! Without closing my eyes, I saw Amber Huntington now the way she looked then, back on that clear Saturday afternoon when we walked the field toward the trailer.

She was telling me all about this book written by a woman doctor who had kept a diary of her patients who had died and then come back to life. While I was thinking about the experience (as described by Amber) of returning from the dead, I heard her sigh a tremendous sigh of relief.

"Does that make you a little less scared of dying?" I had asked.

"Yep! That and being born a Baptist instead of one of them muddleheaded Methodists."

As somebody so far out of it (religiously speaking), I guess I had always sort of assumed that the two local Protestant sects were friendly, seeing as how they were, in our eyes, as similar as Tweedledum and Tweedledee. "Well, I'll be. I sure didn't know," I said, hearing the surprise inside my own voice, "that Baptists and Methodists were all that much different."

Both of Amber's eyebrows immediately arched, and I thought that if she was slapped full force across her face in plain view of the entire Bainesville Regional High School assembly, she wouldn't have looked a bit different from the way she looked at that moment. "Are you kidding!? You're grossing me out!"

"No, I guess I really don't know."

"Well . . ." she said, assuming the air of somebody

who's making the supreme effort at patience, "Baptists can be pretty sure about heaven because they've been *properly* baptized when they were infants. So unless, of course, they go around killing people or stuff like that, then they'll be okay on Judgment Day."

"Methodists get baptized, too. And I know that because Diana Green still has her baptismal dress."

"Ohh no, they don't! What they do is get themselves sprinkled with a few drops of holy water! And that's not what anybody I know would call a *real* baptism. Our minister, Reverend Cantrell, says that being sprinkled is a lot like gambling with one's immortal soul. Have you ever heard of a little sprinkling of rain doing much of anything for dry crops?"

"Uh, no, don't guess I have."

She smiled at me as though I might not be smart, but still I was teachable. "Well, it's the same exact thing with a baptism. Everybody knows that a sprinkling doesn't do the job that a dunking does."

So what would I say to you, Mark? I'd say that we can't be taking it to heart when the majority goes picking on us minorities. After all, those in the majority aren't what you'd call comfortable among themselves. And one thing more, Mark! Any man, and it doesn't much matter how much silver shines in his hair, who's preaching the *true* Gospel of the Prince of Peace wouldn't right now be sowing the seeds of hatred.

21

❦ ❦ ❦ THE RECEPTION honoring us graduates consisted of pink punch in an aluminum bowl, sugar cookies, pimento cheese spread on round crackers, and at least a zillion well-wishers. Still wearing my black robe, I made my way past the refreshment table and through the festive crowd in search of my folks. This was really something! Not since the Bainesville Regional High School played Lorimarr High for the state basketball championship have I seen so many people in one place.

As I edged my way around and through this sometime gym, sometime auditorium, I got to wondering how many came to honor us graduates and how many came to hear the gospel as preached by Jimmy George Johnson? Passing close now to the heavily perspiring minister, who was ringed by three or four layers of admirers, I could, for the first time, see his nose. Actually I could see his whole face, but it was his nose that gave me the start.

Each nostril was as wide as a whole bulb of garlic, and there were a series of miniature red tracks that made a clumsy pattern across the entire width and breadth. Early on Mama taught me to recognize "the drinking man's nose," because that's one of the really important clues that she looks for when giving a reading. "Soon as I see that," she once told me, "I jump right in with my the-world-ain't-yet-learned-to-appreciate-you speech."

Then on the other side of the room I caught a glimpse of hair. Mama's black-as-all-get-out hair! "Now, if you and Pa and the kids just stay put for a minute, I'll come to you," I said under my breath, as I followed a zigzagging path toward them. As I moved closer, I began playing out different variations of the same theme: Mama congratulating me.

In one version both Mama and Papa compete in being the first to give me a hug. And in another Mama's head is tilted slightly as she slowly nods before speaking: "I never in my life had all that much to be proud of, Carol Ann, but I've got something now. And I'm proud, real proud."

When finally I reached the spot where I figured them to

be, they weren't there. Wait! There, over there! I caught another glimpse of her hair, and this time I wouldn't lose them. This time I was only yards away.

So I moved clockwise as quickly as possible around a large cluster of people. There! The back of her head! I came up from behind, grabbing her arm. "Mama!"

She twirled around. Only thing was, the person twirling wasn't Mama! Her eyebrows, which couldn't have been more perfect if they had been painted on, arched like I must be fixing to say something that would explain my surprising action. And that's when I heard myself try. "I was looking for someone else," I said, feeling as though I had said nothing except the obvious. "It's my mother. I know she's here somewhere."

The woman smiled, showing off a perfectly matched set of teeth. "Who is she? Maybe I've seen her. Hardly anybody in Bainesville that I don't know."

"Oh no, that's okay. I think I see her now," I lied. "Over there by the punch bowl," I said as I walked quickly away. But then that wasn't the real reason I didn't say my mother's name, now was it? Sure it is! No . . . no, there's more. You're ashamed of being ashamed, but just the same you're ashamed of the Gypsy! Admit it!

Then, with a tapping on my arm and a vision of Mama in my head, I turned to see an elderly lady pointing a bony finger toward the stage. "The toilets back there?"

"Uh, no ma'am," I said, pointing in the opposite direction. "You have to go out into that hall. Take a right and then go up a ways and you'll find the girls' rest room on your left."

Because she asked me to show her the way, I said that

I'd be glad too; but I wasn't. I slowed my steps down to match her snail's pace. What's another few minutes? It's not as though my folks are going to pick up and take off just because they can't find me right off.

By the time I had escorted her to and from the rest room, the crowd had noticeably thinned out. Most of the people had already watched, congratulated, and eaten, and were now moving toward the door. The party was coming to an end.

Almost frantically, I began moving through the auditorium. She said she'd come. Maybe my graduation wasn't as important to her as I'd like it to be, but just the same, she wouldn't miss it. Mama wouldn't leave me alone, not today! I reached the far end of the room and then I turned and started back.

Calm down, now. Just calm down. There's still a few people in this room I haven't seen, it's not as though I've seen everybody. Faces . . . faces . . . plenty of faces, but still not the right faces. Mama . . . Mama . . . there's been static aplenty between us, but just the same we love each other. Don't we love each other? And don't you know that without you, I'm both alone and lonely?

"Carol Ann!"

With my mother's name already formed upon my lips, I turned. ". . . Oh, Mrs. McCaffrey, hi. I didn't know you were coming here. Are you a fan of Reverend Johnson?"

She broke out into a smile that at least for a moment played with the idea of turning into a full-fledged laugh, but didn't. "Oh, good Lord, no. I think he's a worse ass in person that he is on the tube."

I laughed, too, because for one thing, it wasn't at all like

Mrs. McCaffrey to use a word like that. I mean she just didn't talk that way. But then I guess maybe she did, at least occasionally, in front of a trusted friend. A trusted friend? Me . . . ? Is it possible that I'm that? And that she came here today just to see me graduate? "Uh, you like graduations? Go to many?"

"No, not many, but of course I wanted to see yours. Know something? I was very disappointed that Amber Huntington, and not you, received the most talented award."

"You were?"

She put her arm around my waist. "Well, certainly you deserved it! But let's not be impatient, because someday, hopefully, a whole lot of people are going to be every bit as impressed with your talent as I am."

"Thank you for being here," I said as I looked around at the last of the departing crowd. "Because an accomplishment doesn't much feel like an accomplishment unless somebody . . ." My voice broke under the weight of my words, but I didn't have to finish my thought to have got the meaning across, 'cause Mrs. McCaffrey said, "I know . . . I know." And that was enough to make me understand that she did.

"And this is for you!" she said, raising to eye level a rectangular box covered with polished blue paper and tied with a perfectly enormous white bow.

Just staring at the box helped me realize that I had a friend. ". . . It's wonderful."

"You haven't opened it yet."

"What I mean," I said, knowing that I didn't really have the words right now to explain what I meant, "is that you did this for me." No, I couldn't come close to explaining it; I could only feel it. The pain that comes from Mama giving me nothing and Mrs. McCaffrey giving me something.

"Come on, open it."

"Yes," I said, tearing at the paper without disturbing the bow. But before it was open, she was telling me "to feel free to return it to Feinberg's for anything you want. Even cash."

"Ohh, it's beautiful," I said, fingering the soft cotton dress with the label saying it was made all the way over in India. "How could I ever return something this beautiful?" I felt tears rushing my eyes now, the same tears that I had beaten back only minutes before. I mean she didn't have to give me a thing. But she did. She went and gave me this.

🌷 🌷 🌷

WHEN I WALKED OUT into the early-evening sogginess, there weren't more'n a dozen or so cars and trucks still in the school's parking lot, and Will's truck wasn't among them. I wondered what would happen if a thousand low-flying planes, each trailing a thousand yards of sponges, were sent to dry up all the air over Bainesville?

Where, I asked myself, did I get this really stupid habit of focusing on little things when I have really something important to consider? If anybody, for example, told me that I was about to be blown to dust, I'd probably sit down immediately and try to figure if I'd pulverize into a white, gray, or tan dust and exactly how many ounces I'd weigh.

Any minute now Will, sitting tall behind the wheel of his GMC, will be returning from driving his folks back home, and then he'll be expecting to know exactly what it is that I know. Not a helluva lot. Anyway, why do I have to decide in so few days something as important as marriage? I mean when you get right down to it, Will didn't rush himself before making up his mind that, yes, I really was worth a second date.

Soon as I heard those three light taps of the horn, I knew without looking up that Will had returned. Pushing his head topped by a wavy crop of burnished brown hair through the window, he called, "Hey, lady, waiting for somebody?"

"Uh, yeah, Prince Charming," I answered, as I climbed into the cab next to him. "Seen him around?"

He thumped his chest. "You're looking straight at him, ma'am." Then in a motion so sudden that I didn't have time to prepare my lips, he kissed me. Now with his lips pressing up against mine, I knew that this was right, too, 'cause this was just the way it ought to be. My foolish fears began taking flight, and I knew that I had found a place to be safe. Here between the two strong arms of Will Bellows.

As quickly as he began the kissing, he stopped to put the GMC into drive before announcing, "Hang on to your hat!" And he went driving through the parking lot and onto the street like he was a cowboy after them that rustled his cattle.

A few minutes after Will turned off the highway onto the Jamestown Road, I spotted the blue-and-red neon sign. Although a good many letters had burned out, nobody would have any trouble reading it:

Beul h's Pit Bar-B-Q Ba n
R bs—S ndwi hes—Beans—Be r
"Wh re the elite m et to eat"

He pulled into the oversized dirt parking lot that surrounded Beulah's low-roofed restaurant. "During the Korean War," said Will, "my dad was stationed at the naval shipyard in Boston and he went into this restaurant, right, and he ordered a barbecue sandwich, and know what he got? A fat piece of meat between two slices of white bread and a bottle of barbecue sauce. Yankees don't know the first thing about real pit barbecue."

"Just the same," I told him, "I sure would love to go there. Boston, New York . . . places like that."

"New York might be okay for a visit, but I wouldn't want to live there. Boston might not be all that terrible. At least I could go to Fenway Park when the Atlanta Braves come into town to beat the socks off the Red Sox, right? You like baseball?"

Lying is something that I don't like doing. Besides, when two people are close to marrying, then they've got to be honest. Really get to know one another. I listened for my words of truth, which would have to admit that the only thing that I've found more boring than watching baseball is talking about baseball. Then I looked into a face that was plainly brimming over with enthusiasm for the game, and I answered, "If it's a team I like." Only thing is I've never met a team I liked.

Once we were inside Beulah's, the first thing that struck me was the large size of this knotty-pine room that was decorated with attention-grabbing neon beer signs. This place was a whole lot bigger than the only other two restaurants I've eaten in: Whitman's Cafe and McDonald's.

Finally we located a Formica-topped table next to a jukebox that was as modern as anything. With a sweep of the back of his hand, Will pushed a half dozen empty bottles of Bud, and a couple of ashtrays loaded with cork-tipped stubs, to the far edge of the table. "Only thing I never could stand," he explained, "is other people's messes."

"Neither could I!" I said, joining him in his indignation. Maybe it just helped me feel a bit more justified in always being angry with Mama for being what she is. What she can't help being: a slob.

Then with a look so leisurely that I began to feel uncomfortable, Will studied me. "Hey, you know something?"

"No, what?"

"You look real pretty tonight."

Inside, I felt my temperature soar to about two thousand degrees and I wondered if I was blushing as much on the outside as I was on the inside. "Oh, well . . ." I touched the sleeve of the pale-rose-and-blue dress. "It's just what I'm wearing. I just got it. My graduation gift."

He reached to feel the same spot that I had felt. "It's pretty. Your mother knows what's pretty on you."

"I'm glad you like it. I love it! It was a gift from my music teacher, Mrs. McCaffrey. I didn't even know that she was planning to come to my graduation, but she did. And she brought me this!"

Will scratched the bridge of his nose. "Sounds to me as though she's also the one giving you all the ideas!"

"What do you mean?"

But then the waitress, wearing a blue-and-white checkered polyester uniform with a matching apron, appeared. "What can I get for you folks?"

"I want one of your barbecue pork sandwiches made with dark meat and a Schlitz. What do you want, Carol Ann?"

"Sounds good to me. I'll have the same."

But when she tried to leave without cleaning up the mess, Will called her back. "Hey, you want to wipe up this table?"

Although she made little clicking sounds with her tongue, she *did* clean our table. Anyway, her clicks didn't bother me none. Fact it, I appreciate a man who'll speak up for what's his right. I tried remembering a time when my pa did that, just one time when he stuck up for his rights. But I couldn't, at least not right offhand.

But what was I thinking about him for? Or Mama either for that matter! My eyes took pleasure in the mix of flowers and animals in my new dress. It wasn't my folks who gave me anything, not even—especially not even—the *gift* of their presence.

"You mind," he asked the moment the waitress turned away, "my liking cleanliness and neatness the way I do?"

"Heavens no! I like the way you come right out and ask for what you want in a gentlemanly way, but just the same not taking crap from anybody. Why did you think I minded?"

"Ohh," he said, making a short word into a long one. "Knowing that cleanliness and neatness, seeing as where you come from, don't come all that natural to you."

I felt my anger rip through the soft flesh of my stomach like a sword. "Who do you think gave you the right to speak bad about my folks? Who gave you the right to do that?"

"Hold back a minute, girl, and come on down from your high horse. You're talking to me, right?"

"Answer my question and maybe I'll get off my high horse then, as you call it."

He smiled a smile guaranteed to soften even the hardest of hearts, and besides he sure was good-looking. Maybe not handsome, but just the same, good-looking. "Guess I didn't think anybody in Bainesville, least of all you, needed to be told that your mother wouldn't win no Miss House-keeper of the Year Award."

"I guess I don't need to be told much of anything . . ." I said, swallowing back the tears that were trying like crazy to scale my throat. The funny thing, though, was that I couldn't, offhand, decide who best deserved my anger: Will for saying it or Painter and Gypsy for living it.

He leaned over to place a gentle kiss on my lips. "Hey, there's nothing to be upset about. I'm not marrying your folks, right? I'm marrying you."

"Yes," I answered as I felt the fury begin to subside.

"And I'll tell you something else. If you hadn't sung that day, right, I wouldn't ever have known how special you are."

"You really liked my singing that much?"

"Did I ever!? Are you kidding? Boy, you just up and impressed the bloody hell out of the whole school! Before that there wasn't nobody who thought you had it in you."

"There was one person," I corrected. "Mrs. McCaffrey."

His forehead wrinkled as his mouth took on the look of a mouth that had just bitten into an unripe persimmon. "Oh, her."

"You don't act like you much like her," I said, still

hopeful that I was mistaken. Hopeful that he did, in fact, like her a whole lot.

"Oh, I don't have nothing against her."

I gave his iron jaw a couple of pats, trying to jolly him up as he had, only minutes before, jollied me up. "Why don't you tell me what it is you really think."

"You want to know the one thing I can do without, right, is—"

The waitress returned bearing about a dozen bottles of beer on a round tray. She took two of them off and placed them before us. "Your sandwich won't be ready for a while. The kitchen's all backed up with orders."

Will lifted the bottle, dripping with beads of cold, toward his lips, his warm soft lips. "About how long you think it'll be?"

"Just as soon as the cook catches up," she said, already moving away. "They're all backed up with orders."

When Will replaced the bottle on the table, a good third of the beer had traveled from bottle to belly. "You want to know what I think of Mrs. McCaffrey, right?"

"Yes, I guess I do." But please don't say bad things about her, I thought. Please don't go meddling with my need to feel good about her and have her feel good about me.

With his index finger, he wrote the letter W on the still-sweating neck of his bottle. "Well . . . I personally don't have anything against her. She played the organ for my sister when she got married, right, but . . ."

"But . . ." I repeated. Let's hear what he's got to say. Let's get it over with. Anyway, it couldn't be bad. There's nothing bad that anybody could say about Mrs. McCaffrey.

"But she's got no damn right making you go out and try to do what she wants you to do. And what not one person in a thousand can do."

"You mean trying to make it in the music world?"

"Yeah, how many Elvis Presleys do you think there are in the world? You think it's easy?"

"I never said it was."

"I don't think it's right what Mrs. McCaffrey is trying to do. Getting you all steamed up about something that can't happen. Remember, it's not going to be her out there, busting *her* gut!"

I could almost hear the ripping and tearing of my loyalties. "You got no reason getting mad at Mrs. McCaffrey, Will! She's one person—maybe the only person in this town trying to help me. Trying real hard to help me!"

Looking as though he'd been suddenly slapped across the mouth, Will said, "That so! Who do you, for Christ's sakes, think I am? I'm your sworn enemy, right? If I wasn't trying to help you, I wouldn't have gone and asked you to marry me, now would I?"

"I sort of hoped it was because you liked me. You never once said so, but just the same I hoped that you did."

"Sure I like you! I've liked you ever since that day you sang 'God Bless America.' "

"Yes, but even after that time we went to McDonald's, six months went by and we were never together again. Not till last week."

"Hey, I liked you a lot. The only reason I stayed away was to keep from getting serious."

"You wanted to *keep* from being serious?"

". . . Yeah, well . . . I mean, hey, let's face it! All things being equal, I'd rather marry a girl with the right kind of family, right, like you know what I mean." Will smiled as though now that he explained it, he was kind of pleased by his efforts.

"Yeah, I guess I do." Although I wished it was some other way, I don't too much blame Will for feeling the way he does about my family. "What made you go changing your mind? I mean about getting serious?"

"When I read the story they wrote about you in the paper, you about to go gallivanting around, singing your songs in front of stars and agents and important people like that. I figured if I didn't catch you before you left, then that would be that!"

Probably it was only because I didn't know what to think, and especially not what to say, that I merely repeated, ". . . that would be that."

"Sure, so aren't you glad we're marrying? You can settle down, have a decent life for a change."

My brains felt as though they were being scrambled with Elmer's glue. Did he mean by that that I've lived a wicked life? Or did he mean only that with him, I could be sure of a decent standard of living?

"So," Will said, interrupting my thinking, "aren't you glad we're marrying?"

"I guess I'm not sure right now what I'm glad about, and what I'm not."

He looked as though he was fixing to join me in my confusion. "You mean outside the fact that me and you is fixing to get hitched, right?"

I must have stared at Will for some moments before I

came to believe that somewhere out there, there was a kind of clearing beyond my mental fog. Only thing is that seeing things true meant that I'd have to do what was right for me. But what if what was right wasn't the same thing as what was easy?

"You *were* asked a question," said Will, wearing an expression I hadn't seen before.

"Reckon I know that," I told him. "But I never before had an answer that I could give you. Not until now."

"Two dark-meat barbecues!" sang out the waitress, at the same time she practically slammed the plates onto the table. "There now," she said soothingly. "It didn't take all that long, now did it?"

Will watched her move away as I watched his Adam's apple move up and then down. "You didn't know," he repeated, "until now?"

"No, Will, I guess I didn't. I want to tell you the truth, least the way I see it."

He looked every bit as friendly as a very proud person who suddenly finds himself the butt of a very public joke. "It's about time."

"What I'm trying to tell you . . ." I said, wondering how to make him feel less ripped apart than he already did, "is that your asking me to be your wife was just about the nicest thing that has ever happened to me."

"Yeahyeahyeah . . ."

"I can't talk to you if you do that, act like that."

He looked at me like I looked pitiful enough for the cats to have dragged me in. "If you want to talk, TALK!"

". . . I guess I want to try and explain . . . if I think you're trying to understand."

He took an overly generous bite of sandwich. "I'm not a man that's big on explanations. Give me action or give me nothing. You telling me that you're not going to marry me, right?"

I heard myself sigh. "Yes, I guess maybe I am."

With a brisk wave of his right hand, he seemed to dismiss both me and my words as something of no importance. "Well, don't go worrying your little head about it, honey chile, 'cause I'm going to get by just as nice as you please."

"What?"

"Who in their right mind ever told you that you were the pick of the litter?"

"I don't understand why—"

"I don't understand why," he mimicked. "All I'm doing is telling you not to go feeling all that bad about it. Fact is, you're the one making the mistake, not me!"

"Why can't we leave friends?" I asked, but there was one thing I knew. The confusion was gone. I was doing the right thing.

"Oh, there are other girls around that I can marry, right, lots of them. But I can't for the life of me tell you why anybody in their right mind would want to marry up with the stupid likes of a Delaney!"

"Someday, Will Bellows, you're going to eat those words."

"Me! Eat my words!?" he asked, while showing a mouthful of half-eaten food. "Don't go taking bets on it!"

"I'll take bets on it, all right! 'Cause after I've made it as a singer or a composer or both, I'm coming back to this here town, Will, and you want to know why? Just so I can hear you and Amber Huntington and almost everybody else in Bainesville tell me just how friendly you all were to me back in the good ole days. Back then when you all believed in me and my talent!"

He laughed a laugh that wasn't one bit calculated to sound friendly. "Boy, oh boy, you sure dream a lot, don't you?"

"So what if I do!" I told him. "With my eyes wide open I dream dreams about someday becoming somebody special."

"Yeah? You and everybody else."

"But I will be! Wait and see. Just you wait and see."

I watched his expression change from outright hostility to a kind of puzzlement. "Hey, it wasn't even you that the class picked as most talented, right? I don't understand how you can believe what you do, as strong as you do."

"I only believe what it is I know to be true. I've got the talent and the determination, too. And there's nothing going to stop me, Will. Nothing. Absolutely nothing!"

22

I LEARNED more in the week after I graduated than I have in all the twelve years before. Or at least that's the way it seemed to me. And despite what Mrs. Constant was always saying about "the glories of learning," it sure did have its hurtful side.

Take Mama, for example. I guess I'd known for a lot longer than I wanted to that she wasn't all that . . . all that motherly. But just the same, it was a shock. A bad shock. But because everybody was asleep when Will drove me home on graduation night, I didn't get to talk to my folks about things until the next day, but frankly that was soon enough.

The next morning, as they sat at the table over cigarettes and coffee, I asked, "How come you all didn't come to my graduation?" I expected both Mama and Papa to give me quick excuses that I'd work hard trying to believe, but that's not what happened.

Papa said, "I told you we should've gone Evelyn."

Mama just shrugged as she inhaled her cigarette. "Reckon I just didn't much wanna."

And with those words my old-time fear of being un-loved and uncared for became a towering monster of reality. Even so, I knew now that what I used to believe about their putting the wheels back on the trailer and secretly driving off without me could never come true. No, they needed me too much for that. But just the same there are other ways to desert your kids.

And so it was at that moment, when Mama said that she didn't much want to go to my graduation, that finally I came to understand in all the ways that really mattered that I had been abandoned. That I had long ago been aban-doned. It was at that moment that something between us broke. What was it that broke? Not love, because I didn't exactly stop loving them. No, I guess it was only that I stopped needing them.

❧ ❧ ❧

BECAUSE IT WAS DRIZZLING when I woke, I couldn't too much estimate the time. Probably somewhere

230

about five, maybe five thirty, I thought as I slithered my way to the end of the bed without even the least bit disturbing either Bubba Jay or Alice Faye.

I found the alarm clock sitting on the kitchen table alongside a dozen or so empty cans of beer, the remains of some TV dinners, and a cracked cereal bowl filled to the brim with cigarette butts smoked all the way down to their filters.

It was exactly ten minutes before six A.M., or almost three hours before that Trailways bus would come lumbering down the highway. I dropped yesterday's garbage into a brown paper bag, wiped the table, swept the floor, washed, dried, and put away the dishes, while worrying whether there would ever be a clean dish in the place once I was gone.

By the clock, it was now six fifteen. I washed, dressed, and packed all my belongings inside a plastic shopping bag.

Six twenty-five A.M. Nothing left to do now but write the letter. I took out my old loose-leaf notebook and a yellow pencil marked forever with dozens of imprints of my teeth and began to write:

Dear Mama & Papa,

By the time you read this, I'll be miles away. So I want to try to explain so you'll understand why I'm doing what I'm doing. Maybe if I can explain it good enough, then you'll understand and wish me well.

The closest I can come to explaining why I can't marry Will Bellows and also can't be a part of the Delaney Family Business is that for me it just doesn't feel right. Does *not* feel right!

Okay, so you probably think what does it mean (or matter), this not feeling right? Probably you're saying it's nothing but a bunch of words that don't mean much of nothing.

Guess I can explain it best by telling you something that happened a couple of years back when I was trying on some shoes at the Dixie Bargain Store. Remember when Mr. Granger himself was waiting on us and he told me that the shoes that I wanted to buy were too big and said I ought to buy the same exact shoe, only a half size smaller? Can you remember that?

Well, the 6½ size didn't feel right and I must have used those same words with him at least 4 or 5 times. Once I remember looking him right in the eye and saying, "Mr. Granger, these shoes don't feel right!"

He only laughed, though, while telling me that he had been fitting shoes ever since he was my age (which must have been 14, 'cause that was the age I was then) and if that 6½ was really too small for me then he wouldn't be selling them to me.

Well, they were too small and he did sell them to me, and so for the better part of a year I never took a single step that didn't hurt. Maybe, though, it was a good lesson that I learned on account of those shoes. 'Cause that's when I told myself that I'd never again buy another thing or do another thing that "didn't feel right."

So getting right down to the point, so to speak, marrying Will simply "did not feel right," and neither did becoming a part of the Delaney Family Business.

Now that I've told you what didn't feel right, I want to tell you what does. Making the most of my talents and making the most of me. So I'm going to Nashville to audition for Mrs. McCaffrey's friends at the Blue Note Recording Company. If that doesn't work out, I'm going to try every recording company in Nashville, and anybody in the music business will tell you that there are quite a few in that town. There is also in Nashville The Grand Ole Opry, and there are other things too that might or might not work out.

I know I've told you both a lot of this stuff before, so if I've repeated myself, I'm sorry.

Anyway, I want you to know that I'm going to do everything I know how to do to make a name for myself. If I'm successful (and I sure do aim to be), then I will remember the family and help you all out with money the best I can.

Please tell the kids that I love them. Tell them too that when I come back, I'm going to have *something* for them. For you and Papa too!

Your loving (but not-very-obedient) daughter,

Carol Ann Delaney

soon to be

CARLOTTA DELL

P.S. I've taken 3 $10 bills from the Delaney Family Business as a kind of business loan.

I stuck the pencil between my teeth while I read and reread my letter. My name! Did I hear my name being called? Was Mama calling me? Was she going to wave me to her, explaining that in spite of things done and in spite of things undone, in spite of things said and things left unsaid, she did love me. Always did . . . always would love me.

But on closer listening, it wasn't my name that I heard, but only snores coming from the back of the trailer. So I took the pencil from between my teeth and wrote:

P.P.S. Although I know that I've disappointed you all badly, I hope that it won't change the really important thing. I mean I hope it won't keep you from loving me as much as I have always loved you.

As neatly as I knew how, I folded the letter into quarters before addressing it: Mama & Papa. And then at eye level on the open shelf above the cookstove, I propped it up between a bottle of catsup and a can of black pepper. One more thing! The tape cassette that Miss Thompson was nice enough to let me record yesterday on the school's equipment. Somehow Mama will get ahold of a tape recorder to play it on, and then she sure enough won't need me.

On the label I wrote: Carol Ann singing "Swing Low, Sweet Chariot" and placed it next to the pepper. Standing there senselessly staring at the casette, I suddenly felt flooded by so much emotion. Don't drown . . . don't think. Pepper! Think only about pepper! Where it grows and all the people who make their living from picking it, and all the people who earn their bread from spilling it into those little tin cans.

While keeping myself from looking at the quietly sleeping Bubba Jay and Alice Faye, I placed a Scooter Pie directly above each of their heads. Then I whispered, "Today, no matter what, you're going to have something in your life—at least one thing in your life that's sweet." But could a Scooter Pie, I wondered, ever be sweet enough to wipe away the bitter taste of desertion? But kids, I'm not deserting you . . . I'm only— Pepper! Pepper! Think only of pepper!

I thought of pepper while I was reaching down to pick up my guitar and my bag of belongings, and I even thought of pepper as I stood to face the door. See, you can do it. Do it easy. Easy? I heard myself laugh. "No, not easy. Things that are easy wouldn't hurt as much as this."

Still holding on to my gear, I closed my eyes while saying my last whispered good-bye. "Mama . . . Papa . . . forgive me for doing to you what I grew up fearing you'd do to me." Then I turned the knob, and without even once looking back, I tiptoed out the door.

23

❦ ❦ ❦ UNTIL I WALKED OUT, I didn't know that it was actually drizzling beneath those gunmetal skies. And between the still-unplanted rows of earth, muddy waters moved energetically on like a lot of miniature Mississippis. Although I wasn't there, I know that it must have been a day a lot like today that caused old Noah to draw up plans for his ark.

For moments or maybe minutes, I stood beneath the rain only feet from our trailer door and wondered if today was the right day. I mean wouldn't it make more sense to take my stand on earth that was solid instead of water-logged? And what would be so terrible about slipping back inside, removing the letter and cassette from the shelf, and then quietly sliding back into a warm, dry bed between Bubba Jay and Alice Faye?

Funny, but this time the answer came to me almost as easily as the question. Now that I'd so freshly felt the pain of amputation, I knew that I'd never have the courage to put myself through it, no, not a second time. The time was now . . . or the time was never.

"Never will never do!" I said, taking off in a sprint. To avoid the muddy streams, I began skipping across the top of each row. Hey, that's not bad. Keep the rhythm going. The right foot on top of one row; the left foot on top of the other. Make a game out of it. Right, then left . . . right then left. . . .

By counting the rows my mind was kept almost as occupied as my feet. And then somehow, some way, one stabbing thought squeezed in, and for I don't know how long, I forgot to count. Never forget to count . . . never forget me, Bubba Jay. Stop it! Stop it! Only the count . . . only the toddling around the trailer calling, "Cow, Cow, Cow. . ." No, no, the count . . . no, no, kids, I didn't desert you! And you and Alice Faye are not alone. So eat your Scooter Pies and let the sweetness ooze over everything that's not.

Pepper! Pepper in tin boxes! All the people who pick peppers and all the people who pour them into tin boxes.

Pepper grows on pepper plantations. Coffee grows on coffee plantations and cotton grows on cotton plantations.

My sandals are muddy now, but only a half inch or so above the soles. Once I reach the bus station, I won't have any trouble cleaning them with a few paper towels. Nothing to fret about.

And okay, so my hair is shampoo wet now, too, but that's not any big deal either, 'cause in my belongings bag are ten pink rollers, a plastic bottle of green shampoo, and a trial-size bottle of hair conditioner, the very same brand that Amber and her mother once used on me.

Amber Lee Huntington . . . Amber Lee Huntington . . . the power of those words. Just saying your name makes me feel by comparison as common as a dandelion. Funny how you have me and everybody else believing that you're as special as you pretend to be. Sometimes I wonder, do you believe it? I mean *really* believe it?

But I don't care nothing about that! What I care about is that once she saw me ask for something—how come I didn't know better than to ask for something she could never give? Her friendship. And maybe it was just that act of showing her how much I wanted to be her friend that even now makes me feel angry, ashamed, and naked. Feels like you've seen me without my clothes, Amber. Without a single stitch of my protective covering.

In spite of the rainy, bone-chilling morning, I felt myself perspiring from all the running. Haven't even made it to the highway yet, and I've already found something to regret. Wearing my beautiful gift dress. My only fit-for-audition dress. Didn't I know better than to go and do a dumb thing like that?

But the reason, I reminded myself, wasn't altogether dumb. As a matter of fact, it seemed downright important at the time. 'Cause leaving home, no matter what people think, doesn't only have to do with what you're off in search of. No sir, leaving home has every bit as much to do with what you're leaving behind. And what I had to leave behind was the look of the loser as modeled by the former Miss Carol Ann Delaney. I had to take on the look of somebody who knew something about winning, at least about sometimes winning.

The gully separating the edge of the field from the highway was swollen with fastly flowing rainwater. But with a combination of speed, skill, luck, and a flying leap, I found myself on the opposite side of the road without a single spatter of mud on my audition dress. As I walked the highway's shoulder, I smelled something that reminded me that there were feelings to feel besides pain and longing.

Facing the highway was a brown clapboard house with windows open wide enough to allow the satisfying aroma of frying bacon to escape. That's something I'm going to do once I make it: Always have bacon in my house so I can fry some up anytime I get the notion.

Another thing that'll feel so good I could probably taste it is coming back to this ole town famous. Rich and famous! That's when Amber Huntington is going to try to make me remember those long-ago, good ole Bainesville days when we were such good friends. Chances are that's going to be one of my really important signs that I'm a success. Amber pretending to be . . . wanting to be . . . and, best of all, regretting that she never was my friend.

Inside the bus station there was a solid line of pink

plastic bucket seats facing a long line of vending machines. For the right amount of coins you could buy lipstick, a comb, potato chips, peanut brittle, Fritos, Coke, Pepsi, and among other things an Arkansas road map. In case one of their bus drivers lost his way?

I walked right up to the ticket counter, where a woman whose face I had seen around this town looked up. "Howdy."

"Hi," I answered back. "I'm going to Nashville."

"Nashville?" she asked like she'd never before heard tell of such a place. "Why, honey, you is way early. That bus ain't scheduled till ten minutes before nine."

"Oh, I know that," I told her. "But you see, I still have something to do. Still have somebody to tell good-bye."

❦ ❦ ❦

AT FIRST Mrs. McCaffrey's face showed surprise and then slowly that surprise seemed to give way to understanding. She held the door open for me. "Why, Carol Ann, come on in. You're soaked to the bone. We've got to get you into some dry clothes."

"Oh, it doesn't matter none. They dry sooner or later just from the wearing."

"Go on into the bathroom," she instructed, "and put on that terry-cloth robe that's hanging on the back of the door. Then you can throw your wet clothes into the drier."

While my dress tumbled around, through and over jets of forced hot air, I slid into the kitchen booth.

"It shouldn't take all that long," Mrs. McCaffrey said, glancing toward the drier. Then she cleared her throat. "You've left home, haven't you?"

"I'm going to try my luck in Nashville." But when her face showed no readable expression, I reminded her, "It was you who told me to do it. Told me how talented and all I am! How important it is that I show that talent to all the right people."

"I know . . . I know. I just didn't realize that you'd actually do it like this. In this way. . . ."

She had drifted away. My life raft. And I was alone. All alone, struggling to stay afloat in the midst of a vast and turbulent sea. I asked her, "What do you mean in *this* way? How many ways do you think I have open? And anyway, exactly what's wrong with *my* way?"

She looked up from her hands that she seemed to have been very carefully examining. "It's just that I'm worried about you. Who do you really know in those cities? Who'll take care of you? What do you really know about surviving in big cities? How in God's name will you manage!?"

I heard myself sigh. Sometimes explanations take more energy than almost anything else. "Know something, Mrs. McCaffrey?" I asked, pausing only long enough to put my thoughts into working order. "I know you're wishing me well and I surely do thank you for that. . . ." Although my voice trailed off, my brain was still in motion. Actually, I was gunning my brain as hard as it could go so that I would say the truth in a way that wouldn't be hurtful.

"I think you know," she said when my pause went too long unused, "that you can talk to me."

"Oh, yes ma'am, I know that! But what I have to say I wouldn't want you to take in the wrong way, think that I was criticizing you. There's never been anybody in my life that's been half as good to me as you!"

"All right then," she said, touching the back of my hand and allowing hers to linger there. "If you believe that, and I can tell you do, there's nothing you can tell me that could possibly change the way I feel about you. So please . . ."

"Well . . . it has to do with who you are and who I am. What it is I am. A Gypsy."

"But I already know that," she said, as though there wasn't anything more to discuss.

"Yes, but you don't understand us Gypsies. You see, Mrs. McCaffrey, you were carefully brought up. Carefully educated. And all your life, whether you know it or not, you were ever so carefully taken care of like a . . . like a beautiful greenhouse flower. But with us Gypsies, it's not like that. Not anything at all like that!"

"So. . . ?"

"So we grow up kind of wild . . . kind of free. Learning to read faces and palms long before we're taught to read. Fact is, most of us never learn to read, but we sure as shooting learn how to get by. For example, I can sleep in places too small or too hard for other folks, and sometimes I can even find something to eat when there's nothing to eat.

"Once my grandfather—he was King of the Gypsies, you know—explained it to me. We're an ancient people, we Gypsies, and the reason we've been around so long is that we've learned to survive. And as long as this earth spins, there will always be Gypsies because we carry with us—in our very blood—the ways of surviving."

"Ah," said Mrs. McCaffrey, as though I was about to make sense after all.

Her understanding helped to spur me on. "That's why we do the things we do. Telling the past . . . foretelling the future. And it makes me sick knowing that this is true, but just the same, I know it's true. Gypsies believe that it's okay to steal from non-Gypsies as long as it's something they really need. As bad as I think that this is, it could be worse, 'cause most Gypsies draw the line at stealing out of pure greed. They say it goes against their honor. Well, it goes against my honor to steal anything at all, but just the same, I know I won't go hungry."

"Then you're telling me," she said, wearing an expression that seemed part admiration, part fascination, "that you're going to be fine."

I grabbed her hand and squeezed it. "That's it! Believe in me, please, because that's exactly it. I'm going to be fine. Just fine."

❦ ❦ ❦

THE RAIN had stopped, and there, hanging resolutely over the Bainesville sky, was an honest-to-goodness rainbow. As I was walking the four or five blocks back to the bus station, I kept fingering the letters of introduction to Mrs. McCaffrey's sorority sisters just to make sure that they stayed safe and dry. Even Gypsy luck can use all the help it can get.

And as I walked, I never once lost sight of that rainbow. Just eyeing that rainbow and humming. At first I was only humming the music to one of my own songs, but soon I was really singing it. Words and music.

"Hey, cut that out!" I told myself. "Didn't anybody ever tell you that folks who sing to themselves on the street look every bit as daffy as people who talk to themselves?"

And yet even with my very sensible warning, I went right on singing. My heart, at least, seemed to understand that singing was something that I needed to do, even though my head was just too ramrod rigid to understand that music can sometimes give a person some badly needed courage. You think it's an accident that bagpipes, tomtoms and military bands are part of the weapons of war?

Inside the waiting room a few people lounged awkwardly in bucket-back chairs while a small boy, not much older than my Bubba Jay, pulled one vending machine knob after another.

I walked over to the ticket window, and without waiting to hear my question, the lady answered it. "It oughta be coming along pretty soon now, honey." So I went back outside to wait . . . and to sing.

> *"In a land where no one ever goes,*
> *Where water never flows,*
> *There grows a flower,*
> *One wild, wild flower.*
> *People ask,*
> *Can this be so?*
> *But only the flower,*
> *The wild, wild flower, really knows.*
> *Yes, it really knows."*

BETTE GREENE is the author of *Summer of My German Soldier*, an ALA Notable Book, a National Book Award finalist, and a 1973 *New York Times* Outstanding Book of the Year; *Philip Hall likes me. I reckon maybe.*, a 1975 Newbery Honor Book and a 1974 *New York Times* Outstanding Book of the Year; *Morning Is A Long Time Coming* and *Get on out of here, Philip Hall.*

Ms. Greene grew up in a small Arkansas town and later moved to Memphis, Tennessee, and then to Paris. She now lives in Brookline, Massachusetts, with her husband and their two teenagers, Carla and Jordan.